Schriften
des
Vereins für Socialpolitik.

130. Band. Vierter Teil.

Gemeindebetriebe.

Neuere Versuche und Erfahrungen über die
Ausdehnung der kommunalen Tätigkeit in Deutschland
und im Ausland.

Dritter Band.

Vierter Teil.

Leipzig,
Verlag von Duncker & Humblot
1910.

Gemeindebetriebe
in
Frankreich und England.

Von

H. Berthélemy, und **Douglas Knoop,**
Paris, Manchester.

Der Gemeindebetriebe dritter Band. Vierter Teil.

Im Auftrag des Vereins für Socialpolitik
herausgegeben von
Carl Johannes Fuchs.

Leipzig,
Verlag von Duncker & Humblot.
1910.

Alle Rechte vorbehalten.

Piererſche Hofbuchdruckerei Stephan Geibel & Co. in Altenburg.

Inhaltsverzeichnis.

                                                                                Seite

I. Les Industries Communales en France. Par H. Berthélemy   1
II. The Trading Enterprises of Manchester. By Douglas Knoop 15

Les Industries Communales en France.

Par

H. Berthélemy,
Professeur de droit administratif à l'Université de Paris.

Le développement du „Socialisme municipal" est un fait universel. Les causes générales de ce mouvement se sont fait sentir en France comme partout ailleurs. L'opinion publique, cependant, s'y montre habituellement assez peu favorable à l'extension des industries communales.

Ce sentiment de défiance tient, croyons-nous, à deux raisons qui d'ailleurs s'expliquent l'une par l'autre. C'est le caractère politique de nos institutions communales; c'est en second lieu le recrutement démocratique des administrateurs municipaux.

Le caractère politique des institutions communales en France n'est pas voulu par nos lois; il s'est implanté dans nos moeurs.

Les lois donnent strictement aux représentants de la cité les pouvoirs qu'il faut pour gérer utilement les services d'intérêt collectif: police, hygiène, écoles, cimetières, voirie, marchés, abattoirs, etc. . . . Il n'existe aucun rapport visible entre les mesures à prendre sur ces différentes matières et l'opinion politique des gens qu'on chargera de prendre ces mesures. Les voeux politiques sont même interdits aux conseils municipaux. Et cependant ces conseils apparaissent d'un bout à l'autre de la France, dans nos grandes villes et dans nos villes moyennes, comme de véritables assemblées politiques bien plus que comme des conseils d'administration. On s'y fait élire pour son opinion et non pour son aptitude.

Ayant pris ainsi la physionomie d'un premier échelon dans la hiérarchie des mandats politiques, les fonctions municipales sont recherchées par les petites gens, ambitieux de s'en faire un tremplin pour parvenir à de hautes destinées. Dans un grand nombre de villes, même importantes, les conseillers municipaux sont en majorité des artisans ou des ouvriers.

Composées de la sorte, nos assemblées communales manquent presque toujours des qualités nécessaires à la conduite d'une grande exploitation industrielle ou commerciale.

Les municipalités qu'elles élisent ne semblent ni plus habiles ni moins suspectes. Les entreprises que les circonstances particulières ont placées entre leurs mains sont habituellement gérées sans économie. Les emplois inutiles y sont multipliés, proie alléchante pour les parasites des partis victorieux. La discipline des services s'y ressent de la nécessité pour les chefs, de ménager le personnel. On manque d'autorité à l'égard de ceux dont on dépend, et les conseillers municipaux dépendent des suffrages de ceux dont ils utilisent les services. Un maire ne blâmera pas, ne révoquera ou ne suspendra pas un commis infidèle ou négligent avec la même fermeté qu'y mettrait un patron personnellement intéressé à la marche d'une grande entreprise.

Notre système législatif a été influencé par cette méfiance à l'égard des administrations communales. Notre jurisprudence s'en est de même inspirée et ce n'est qu'avec de très prudentes réserves et dans des hypothèses particulièrement favorables qu'elle a admis la création ou l'extension des services industriels exploités en régie par les administrateurs communaux.

Ce sont là deux points qu'il est intéressant de préciser.

Les industries municipales devant la loi.

De jeunes professeurs de talent n'ont pas craint d'affirmer qu'aucune loi française ne faisait obstacle à la création et à l'exploitation directe par les communes des services industriels.

Les communes, disent-ils, jouissent de la personnalité morale. Or les personnes morales n'ont pas moins d'aptitudes que les personnes physiques, à qui elles sont intégralement assimilées. Toute personne peut tout ce qui n'est pas défendu par les lois. Aucune loi n'a dit que la personne „commune" serait frappée d'incapacité quant à la gestion directe des services d'intérêt général. C'est donc à tort, et par un excès de prévoyance où l'on peut voir un abus ou un détournement de la tutelle administrative, que les autorités supérieures (Conseil d'état ou ministres) ont, toutes les fois que cela leur a semblé possible, fait obstacle à la municipalisation des services publics.

On a même été jusqu'à taxer d'incohérente la jurisprudence du Conseil d'État sous prétexte que, sans adopter aucune règle fixe, elle se laisse guider par les circonstances de fait et de lieu pour se montrer favorable ou non aux entreprises des municipalités.

Nous estimons que le Conseil d'Etat est au contraire demeuré parfaitement logique et respectueux de la loi.

Il est bien vrai de dire que toute personne, même morale, peut tout ce qui ne lui est pas défendu. Il faut cependant renverser la proposition quand il s'agit de services publics, même généraux. Il faut dire: aucun service, agissant avec les deniers publics, gérant les affaires publiques, n'est compétent que dans les limites qui lui sont assignées par les lois.

C'est une maxime fondamentale du droit public français que la loi seule est souveraine. Or les lois n'ont investi aucun service d'une compétence générale et absolue. Il n'existe aucune autorité dont on puisse dire que pour le bien public, elle peut tout, sauf ce qui lui est interdit.

C'est là le sens véritable et profondément libéral du grand principe de la spécialité. On en méconnaît singulièrement la portée lorsqu'on veut n'y voir qu'une règle mesquine ayant pour but d'interdire aux établissements publics l'acceptation de dons et legs faits avec une affectation étrangère à leur objet normal.

Telle est bien, sans doute, dans tout le cours du XIXe siècle, l'application la plus fréquente qui a été faite de ce principe. Il n'était pas possible d'autoriser la délivrance des legs charitables ou scolaires faits aux fabriques paroissiales, puisque les dites fabriques n'avaient exclusivement pour but que l'administration des biens cultuels.

Mais il faut regarder plus haut qu'une application particulière pour apercevoir le principe qui la commande. Or ce principe, applicable à tous les services publics, à tous les fonctionnaires publics, a une portée très générale: c'est, à savoir, qu'aucun agent d'aucun service n'est investi d'une compétence illimitée; c'est qu'en dehors des besognes assignées et des actes formellement permis aux agents des différentes administrations publiques, tout ce qui se fait au nom de l'intérêt général et avec les deniers publics est illégalement accompli.

Il s'agit bien ici de la capacité plus ou moins complète des personnes morales! Oui, certes, elles sont pleinement capables:

mais le fait qu'en tant que personne morale l'établissement ou le service peut être sujet de droit aussi largement qu'un simple particulier, ce fait, disons-nous, n'implique aucunement que les fonctionnaires chargés de l'administration du service soient maîtres d'agir à leur guise.

C'est bien à tort qu'on prétend distinguer ici entre les services spécialisés et ceux qui ont un rôle apparemment général. Sans doute la controverse serait impossible s'il s'agissait d'un établissement public tel qu'une université, un bureau d'assistance ou un hôpital. La vérité c'est qu'il n'existe aucun service administratif qui n'ait une compétence limitée. La reconnaissance de la personnalité morale à un service quel qu'il soit, augmente bien sa capacité, mais n'augmente pas ses attributions.

Or la question de l'aptitude des communes à créer et à gérer des services industriels ou commerciaux n'est pas une question de capacité: c'est une question d'attributions. Les attributions des conseils municipaux et des municipalités sont définies par la loi du 5 Avril 1884. Comprennent-elles ou ne comprennent-elles pas, ou dans quelle mesure comprennent-elles la faculté d'exploiter en régie des services industriels? C'est le problème posé.

La solution n'en est pas avancée par la constatation que les communes sont des personnes morales.

L'art. 61 de la loi municipale dit que le Conseil „règle par ses délibérations les affaires de la commune". Nous n'en pouvons rien déduire, car il faudrait encore avoir une définition précise de ce que sont „les affaires de la commune". L'exploitation d'une boulangerie, d'une épicerie, d'une mercerie municipale constitue-t-elle une „affaire de la commune"? Dira-t-on que les affaires de la commune sont toutes les opérations que l'intérêt général justifie? — Mais encore faudrait-il établir qu'il est conforme à l'intérêt général d'avoir une boulangerie municipale plutôt que plusieurs boulangeries privées, travaillant sous le régime économique de la concurrence!

Aucune autre règle écrite dans la loi ne justifie la création d'industries municipales par délibération du Conseil. Et nous en devons conclure que ce n'est qu'à titre exceptionnel que les communes peuvent être autorisées à créer et à gérer des exploitations industrielles ou commerciales.

Cette solution, au surplus n'est-elle pas seule compatible avec les principes généraux de notre régime municipal, avec les règles de la tutelle administrative, avec le formalisme assez étroit qui domine l'activité des administrations décentralisées? La commune ne peut pas faire comme elle veut ce qu'elle a le droit de faire; comment peut-on soutenir qu'elle a le droit de faire ce qu'elle veut?

Si les hypothèses où l'exploitation d'industries municipales peut être autorisée sont exceptionelles, comment sont justifiées ces exceptions? Comment et par l'effet de quelles causes paraissent-elles susceptibles de se multiplier? C'est, en dernière analyse, à cette dernière formule que se ramène en France le problème du socialisme municipal.

Les communes françaises exploitent un certain nombre de monopoles légaux prévus par des dispositions spéciales et justifiés par des considérations diverses.

Citons ainsi le monopole des pompes funèbres, jadis attribué aux établissements des différents cultes reconnus, et constitué en service public communal par la loi du 28 Décembre 1904. — Citons également l'exploitation, ou plutôt l'aménagement d'abattoirs publics (ord. du 15 Avril 1838). Il ne s'agit pas ici d'un bénéfice à réaliser, mais d'un service à organiser dans les conditions hygiéniques les moins défavorables. Les redevances imposées à ceux qui usent des abattoirs ne doivent pas excéder ce qui est nécessaire pour pourvoir à l'entretien de ces établissements. Citons encore le monopole du pesage, jaugeage et mesurage public (Déc. du 27 Brum. an VII).

En dehors de ces hypothèses qui ne donnent lieu à aucune controverse, les communes ne sont compétentes pour exploiter des entreprises industrielles ou commerciales que lorsque l'utilité publique de ces régies est rendue incontestable par des circonstances locales, notamment lorsque les mêmes services ne peuvent être procurés par l'initiative privée, — ou bien lorsque la création des services dont il s'agit peut être considérée comme se rattachant à l'exercice de la police, — ou bien enfin lorsqu'il s'agit de mettre en valeur le patrimoine communal.

Ce sont ces considérations diverses qui selon notre jurisprudence fort raisonnable et très exactement respectueuse de la loi, peuvent justifier la création ou l'extension des régies municipales.

Les industries municipales devant la jurisprudence.

La jurisprudence dont nous parlons ici est principalement celle du Conseil d'Etat, appelé à exercer sur les actes les plus importants des administrations municipales un contrôle indirect et occasionnel.

Il arrive fréquemment qu'une industrie municipale ne peut être constituée qu'à l'aide de capitaux d'emprunt. Or certains emprunts ne peuvent être contractés qu'avec l'autorisation d'un décret pris en Conseil d'Etat. Le Conseil d'Etat invité à donner un avis se montre défavorable à l'emprunt et entrave de la sorte la tentative.

Souvent aussi le Conseil d'Etat intervient à un autre titre. Les particuliers lésés dans leurs intérêts par les mesures que prennent les administrations municipales ont le droit de demander au Conseil, juridiction administrative supérieure, l'annulation des décisions contraires à la loi. Les commerçants ou industriels qui subissent un dommage du fait de l'institution d'industries ou de commerces concurrents peuvent se pourvoir. On admet même, depuis quelques années, que le pourvoi d'un simple contribuable de la commune est recevable, puisque les contribuables sont manifestement intéressés à ce que les deniers publics affectés aux services municipaux soient gérés parcimonieusement.

Les préfets, enfin, chargés de veiller à l'observation des lois par les assemblées municipales peuvent provoquer l'annulation administrative des délibérations illégales.

Comment ces différents pouvoirs sont-ils exercés?

Les entreprises municipales les plus importantes qui se soient développées, — ou qui sont présentement en voie de se développer sont celles qui, exigeant l'utilisation des voies publiques, ne peuvent jamais être exploitées que sous forme de monopole. Ce sont les industries d'adduction d'eau, de gaz ou d'électricité.

L'installation d'un régime de distribution d'eau s'est toujours faite, jusqu'à présent, sous forme de concession de travaux publics. Une compagnie se charge de l'aménagement des conduites d'eau; elle se rémunère par l'exploitation du service aux conditions fixées par le cahier des charges. Cette exploitation n'est ni très compliquée, ni susceptible de grandes modifications ultérieures. Lorsqu'arrive le terme fixé par le marché, la ville est propriétaire des appareils; l'administration municipale se trouve alors naturellement tentée de se substituer aux concessionnaires et de conserver pour la caisse communale, l'intégralité des bénéfices à réaliser.

Il n'y a pas ici atteinte à la liberté du commerce puisqu'aucune concurrence n'est possible. Il n'y a généralement qu'à suivre les errements et à se conformer aux habitudes introduites par les exploitants. Le personnel de l'exploitation industrielle devient, en bloc, personnel municipal, et l'on passe sans heurt du régime de la concession au système de la régie.

Cela n'a présenté aucune difficulté même dans les grandes villes, et depuis longtemps déjà, sans qu'on ait lieu de s'en plaindre, les deux plus grandes villes de France, Paris et Lyon, ont donné l'exemple.

Avec beaucoup plus de résistance, des motifs analogues ont fait admettre la régie du gaz dans quelques villes moyennes ou dans les petites villes. Les grandes villes, où l'exploitation de cette industrie est beaucoup plus compliquée et se trouve susceptible de très gros progrès, n'ont ordinairement pas été autorisées à exploiter en régie l'éclairage au gaz, même avec des appareils leur appartenant.

Pour la ville de Paris, le Parlement, qui devait être consulté à raison de l'importance des emprunts à faire, ne s'est pas prêté au système de la régie.

Cependant la régie du gaz est réclamée avec insistance par un grand nombre de personnes qui, sur ce point particulier croient avoir de sérieux motifs de ne pas se laisser dominer par le sentiment de défiance dont j'ai parlé plus haut. C'est que trop souvent, les Compagnies du gaz ont abusé, très légalement d'ailleurs, mais très durement cependant, d'un monopole dont les conditions ont, avec le progrès scientifique, considérablement varié. Des procès sans nombre en sont issus; les consommateurs, parfois, se sont coalisés pour faire grève et mettre en péril les bénéfices des compagnies trop exigeantes.

Aussi les villes ont-elles été plus prudentes lorsqu'elles ont concédé l'installation de l'éclairage électrique. Elles ont même, le plus souvent, commis une faute inverse; par crainte des abus de monopoles qui eussent pu assurer au moins le bas prix de l'éclairage ou de la force, elles ont réservé contractuellement des possibilités de concurrence qui sont en fait presque impossibles.

L'eau, le gaz, l'électricité sont des industries qui très logiquement, sont considérées comme échappant à l'inaptitude des villes d'entreprendre des exploitations industrielles.

Nous sommes en présence, ici, de monopoles obligés. Cela seul suffirait pour qu'on put invoquer en faveur de la municipalisation sinon des raisons déterminantes, du moins de sérieuses excuses. Il faut ajouter cette double considération que ces industries exigent toutes l'aménagement du domaine communal; que toutes, elles rentrent dans les mesures de police puisque la police comprend tout ce qu'exige la sécurité et la salubrité de la ville.

Des motifs analogues auraient pu justifier les entreprises municipales de transports en commun. Jusqu'à présent cependant nous ne connaissons pas de villes françaises où les omnibus et tramways soient exploités en régie.

C'est par des raisons toutes différentes qu'on peut expliquer l'existence, dans quelques grands centres, de théâtres ou de casinos municipaux. Il ne s'agit pas tant ici de réaliser des bénéfices ou de faire concurrence aux entreprises privées que d'encourager les arts et que de procurer aux habitants, au prix même de sacrifices, des satisfactions d'ordre intellectuel considérées comme indispensables dans toute agglomération importante.

Le plus souvent d'ailleurs, les théâtres ou casinos municipaux sont concédés ou affermés. L'intervention communale ne se manifeste que par la subvention accordée — toujours nécessaire, et d'ailleurs rarement suffisante, — au moins lorsqu'il s'agit de théâtres proprement dits.

L'avenir du socialisme municipal.

Y a-t-il lieu de désirer l'extension des régies municipales, au moins dans les cas exceptionnels où la loi et la jurisprudence françaises les admettent?

Nous avons dit pour quels motifs on voyait avec méfiance les autorités municipales se charger de fonctions auxquelles la loi ne les a pas destinées. Bien que nous croyions cette défiance très légitime, nous sommes prêts à reconnaître que de sérieuses raisons militent en faveur de la municipalisation de certains services. Nous voulons parler de ceux qui ne se peuvent convenablement exploiter qu'en forme de monopoles.

Il n'y a pas une différence sensible entre l'exploitation d'un réseau de chemin de fer par l'Etat ou par un concessionnaire, et des individualistes déterminés ont cessé de condamner la nationalisation des transports par voie ferrée. On peut, pour des raisons analogues ne pas condamner l'exploitation en régie des entreprises d'eau, de gaz ou d'électricité. On ne peut, pour ces exploitations, rien attendre d'un régime de concurrence qui multiplierait sans profit les frais généraux. Même en matière de distribution de force électrique, on ne peut concevoir, sans danger pour la sécurité publique qu'un très petit nombre d'industries concurrentes installant leurs conduites dans le sous-sol des voies. Il est beaucoup plus avantageux de ne faire qu'une seule fois, dans les meilleures conditions possibles, les travaux coûteux d'installation de câbles électriques, et d'attendre d'un seul service convenablement dirigé l'utilisation générale des forces aménagées.

Signalons à cet égard, pour n'en pas féliciter le Parlement français, l'erreur contraire commise en 1906, lorsqu'on rédigea la grande loi sur les distributions d'énergie électrique.

Cédant manifestement à la pression des ingénieurs ou des producteurs d'électricité, on a édicté des dispositions qui prohibent aussi étroitement qu'on a pu la monopolisation des industries de distribution d'énergie. C'est rendre impossible, — au moins dans cette mesure, — l'un des monopoles municipaux qui aurait pu le mieux se justifier puisqu'il y va tout à la fois de la sécurité et de la commodité des voies publiques.

En définitive les industries que les progrès scientifiques ont amenées à n'être exploitées que socialement seront vraisemblablement considérées dans un avenir plus ou moins éloigné comme rentrant dans le domaine propre des municipalités.

En face des grands monopoles, le consommateur n'est pas garanti par la concurrence. Qui le défendra contre l'exagération des prix sinon l'autorité publique? Et si l'autorité doit légitimement intervenir n'est-il pas plus simple de la charger de pourvoir elle-même à l'exploitation des services dont il s'agit? N'a-t-on pas plus de chance, par ce procédé, d'obtenir une exploitation moins exigeante, moins âpre au gain, plus souple, plus disposée à tenir compte des progrès et plus pressée surtout d'en faire profiter le public?

L'exemple déjà cité de ce qui s'est passé pour l'exploitation du gaz l'a démontré. Les contrats qui stipulaient jadis des prix élevés, — 30 ou 35 centimes le mètre cube de gaz, — semblaient à peine rémunérateurs. Très vite cependant d'immenses progrès ont permis aux compagnies de réaliser de tels bénéfices sur la vente des sous-produits que les frais de fabrication se trouvaient presque couverts. Les actions des compagnies ont pourtant monté dans des proportions énormes, — et le prix du gaz, stipulé contractuellement pour un terme très long n'a pas été diminué. Il n'est pas douteux qu'exploitée en régie, l'industrie gazière aurait abandonné aux consommateurs la plus grosse part, sinon la totalité de ces bénéfices inattendus.

A mesure qu'expirent les concessions accordées, nous devons nous attendre à voir se développer le régime de l'exploitation en régie des industries monopolisées; et nous n'avons pas lieu de regretter cet état de choses: fussent-elles même un peu moins bien conduites, il vaut mieux pour tous que ces industries soient exploitées pour le service à rendre que pour le profit à faire, — autrement dit, pour l'intérêt général plutôt que pour l'avantage de quelques actionnaires.

Ajoutons cependant, — ceci n'est pas sans intérêt puisque cette note a pour objet essentiel la comparaison de ce qui se passe en France avec ce qui se fait chez nos voisins — que notre pays sera l'un des plus lents à pratiquer d'une manière générale ce qu'on nomme, peut-être à tort, le socialisme municipal.

Cela tient aux vestiges du système de centralisation administrative qui a été plus accentué en France que partout ailleurs. C'est notamment le résultat de la tutelle administrative très rigoureuse encore et qui rend trop de services pour que nous soyons près d'y renoncer.

Nous indiquons en terminant quelques ouvrages ou articles où la question des industries municipales est traitée avec beaucoup de précision et de compétence.

Le plus complet est la thèse de M. Pierre Mercier: „Les exploitations municipales commerciales et industrielles en France." (1905.)

De M. Capitant, professeur agrégé à la faculté de Droit de Paris: „L'exploitation municipale des services de distribution de l'eau, du gaz et de l'énergie électrique à Grenoble", dans les questions pratiques de législation ouvrière, 1905 p. 40. — (La régie du gaz existe à Grenoble depuis 1866.)

De M. Gabriel-Louis-Jaray, auditeur au Conseil d'Etat: „Industries municipalisées", dans les questions de législation ouvrière, 1903, p. 106 et 234.

Du même auteur, „le Socialisme municipal en France", annales des Sciences politiques, 1905, p. 189 et suiv.

De M. H. Nézard, professeur agrégé à la faculté de droit de Caen, „La municipalisation du service de l'éclairage public et la ville de Paris", dans la „Revue des sciences et de législation financière", 1905, p. 296 (Article très sérieusement documenté).

De M. E. Bouvier, professeur à la faculté de droit de Lyon: „La municipalisation des services publics devant la loi et la jurisprudence françaises". Comptes-rendus de l'association française pour l'avancement des sciences. Congrès de 1906.

The Trading Enterprises of Manchester.

By

Douglas Knoop,
University of Manchester.

The trading enterprises of the City of Manchester are as important as, if not more important than, those of any other local authority in the United Kingdom. All the most usual municipal trades, the supply of water, of gas and of electricity and the tramways, are owned and managed by the town, which provides water, light, power, heat and transport facilities not only to its own citizens, but also to several hundred thousand more persons residing in neighbouring townships. The sizes and populations of the various areas of supply differ for each service, being largest in the case of water, where about one and a quarter million people, or almost twice the population of the city itself, are supplied. Other branches of municipal enterprise are the ownership and operation of markets, slaughter-houses and cold storage warehouses, the paving of streets and the laying of sewers, the ownership of working-class flats and houses, the management of two large estates in connection with the important municipal cleansing department, the administration of numerous baths and wash-houses and the provision of cemeteries. The largest financial undertaking of a trading character in which the City is interested, is the Manchester Ship Canal Company, in which the local authority holds £ 5 000 000 in debentures and more than £ 1 000 000 in preference shares, and further has the right of appointing ten of the nineteen members of the board of directors. A detailed account of each of the economic activities of the town may now be given [1].

---

[1] This article is based almost entirely upon the printed reports, financial statements and other information kindly supplied by the various municipal departments concerned. To a small extent reference has been made to the National Civic Federation Report on Municipal and Private Operation of Public Utilities (New York, 1907), Part 11, Volume 11, and to the Municipal Year Book for 1909 (London, 1909).

Water Supply.

The water, which the municipality provides, is obtained from two distinct sources of supply. From 1855 onwards, water has been obtained from the Longdendale Reservoirs, whilst the Thirlmere supply did not commence until 1894. Each scheme will be described separately before the water supply as a whole is dealt with.

Longdendale Reservoirs. These are situated in the Pennine Range of hills, close to the source of the River Etherow, on the main Great Central Railway Line from Manchester to Sheffield and London. They lie in the administrative County of Derbyshire, and Woodhead, the village at the head of the reservoir furthest away from Manchester, is 18 miles from that city. The scheme comprises seven reservoirs, erected by damming the Etherow and its tributaries. Their names, area, capacity, depth and height of top water level above ordnance datum are indicated in the following table:

Name of Reservoir	Area	Capacity	Depth	Height of Top Water Level above Ordnance Datum.
	Acres	Gallons	Feet	Feet
Woodhead . . .	135	1 181 000 000	71	782
Torside	160	1 474 000 000	84	651
Rhodes Wood . .	54	500 000 000	68	574
Vale House . . .	63	343 000 000	40	503
Bottoms	50	407 000 000	48	486
Arnfield	39	209 090 000	52	540
Hollingworth . .	13	73 000 000	52	555

The Manchester Royal Exchange is 120 feet above ordnance datum, and the altitude of the highest points in the supply area does not exceed 350 feet.

On leaving Longdendale the water passes through the Mottram tunnel, some two miles long, into the small Godley Reservoir and thence through mains into the large storage reservoirs at Denton, Audenshaw, Gorton and Prestwich some 4 or 5 miles to the north and west of Manchester, details of which are as follows:

Name of Reservoir	Area	Capacity	Depth	Height of Top Water Level above Datum.
	Acres	Gallons	Feet	Feet
Godley	15	61 000 000	21	478
Denton, No. 1 . .	7	30 000 000	20	321
Denton, No. 2 . .	6	23 000 000	20	321
Audenshaw, No. 1	80	528 000 000	27^1/$_2$	340
Audenshaw, No. 2	69	371 000 000	22^1/$_2$	323
Audenshaw, No. 3	102	542 000 000	22^1/$_2$	323
Gorton, Upper . .	34	123 000 000	26	259
Gorton, Lower . .	23	100 000 000	29	244
Prestwich, No. 1 .	4^1/$_2$	20 000 000	22	352
Prestwich, No. 2 .	4^1/$_2$	21 000 000	24	352

Thus the total area of the 17 Reservoirs comprised under the scheme is 859 acres, and the total capacity is 6 006 000 000 gallons.

The drainage ground of the Longdendale Reservoirs is 19 300 Statute acres and its altitude is between 486 and 2060 feet; the rainfall at the uppermost reservoir, where it is always greatest, has on a few occasions, during the last 54 years, exceeded 60 inches per annum. On the other hand, during 1887 it fell as low as 29 inches. The average annual rainfall, for a period of years, at the different reservoirs, was as follows:

Name of Reservoir	Elevation of Rain Guages above Ordnance Datum	No. of Years to which averages refer	Average Annual Rainfall
	feet	years	inches
Prestwich	375	36	34,43
Gorton	263	54	31,75
Denton	324	54	31,56
Godley	500	54	32,62
Arnfield	550	34	38,93
Rhodes Wood	520	54	43,72
Torside	680	44	44,60
Woodhead	660	54	48,60

During the "seventies" of last century, the authorities began to recognise that it was absolutely necessary to provide a new source of supply, capable of extension, to meet the steadily growing demand of the area supplied by the Manchester Corporation. With a view to securing adequate supplies, the Manchester Waterworks' Engineers prepared the scheme by which the city was to obtain water from Lake Thirlmere, situated in the Cumberland hills, some 96 miles North North West of Manchester. The need of a new source of supply was emphasised in the "eighties" by three serious droughts, on each of which occasions the water supply proved to be inadequate. After much opposition the necessary Parliamentary sanction was obtained for the new scheme, and the first contract was let in 1885.

The natural area of Lake Thirlmere was 330 acres and its altitude above sea level was 533 feet. In order to increase the capacity of the lake, it was necessary to raise its level, which was done by means of an embankment constructed at the outlet of the lake into the St. John's Beck. The embankment is 857 feet long and it raised the level of the lake some 35 feet, thereby increasing its area to 690 acres. Ultimately, the level of the lake will be raised another 15 feet to 584 ft. above sea level; its area will then be 793 acres and its capacity 8135 million gallons. At present the lake has a capacity of 5129 million gallons. The aqueduct from Thirlmere to Manchester is constructed to convey 50 million gallons a day. The length is $95^7/_8$ miles and is composed of $14^1/_8$ miles of tunnels, $36^3/_4$ miles of cut and cover and 45 miles of pipes. Originally only one line of pipes was laid, this bringing the first Thirlmere water to Manchester in October 1894. The inauguration of the laying of the second line of pipes took place in October, 1900, whilst water was first supplied through this second line of pipes in November, 1904. In the autumn of 1908 the work of laying the third line of pipes was begun. The cost of the watershed and lake, of the way-leave for the tunnels and cut and cover, and of five lines of syphon pipes across the valleys between Thirlmere and Manchester, and of the construction of all the tunnels and cut and cover to convey 50 million gallons per day, and two lines of pipes to convey 20 million gallons per day, amounts to about three and a half million pounds. When the five lines of pipes have all been laid and the lake raised 50 feet, it is estimated that the cost will be about £ 5 000 000.

The natural drainage area to the lake is 7400 acres, but an additional drainage of 3600 acres will hereafter be diverted into the lake. The rainfall over the drainage area is considerably in excess of that at Longdendale. It varies at different points on the watershed, the average for the last 32 years, as measured by six different guages, being 86,6 inches per annum. The highest average annual rainfall during the years 1877 to 1908 inclusive was 127,4 inches in 1903 and the lowest average annual rainfall was 61,6 inches in 1887.

The average quantity of water supplied per day by the Manchester Corporation Waterworks, has grown steadily, with slight fluctuations, from 8 million gallons in 1855 to 40 million gallons in 1908. The highest average daily consumption before the opening of the first pipe from Thirlmere was 24 million gallons in 1892. Statistics for the last ten years are given in the table which follows:

Year	Average quantity of water supplied per day.		
	Longdendale.	Thirlmere.	Total.
	gallons	gallons	gallons
1899	24 818 280	7 621 613	32 439 893
1900	24 202 660	8 092 298	32 294 958
1901[1]	21 992 260	8 353 284	30 275 544
1902	23 307 915	8 169 011	31 476 926
1903	25 428 747	7 323 814	32 752 561
1904[2]	23 329 099	9 665 482	32 994 581
1905	18 525 187	16 694 391	35 219 578
1906	20 308 534	16 707 579	37 016 113
1907	21 273 143	17 063 973	38 337 116
1908	21 953 321	18 088 130	40 041 451

The Manchester Corporation supplies water to a large number of districts outside the City boundary. The most important is the County Borough of Salford, to which water is supplied in bulk. Smaller townships, which receive a supply in detail, are Barton Moss, Broughton, Carrington, Davyhulme, Denton, Droylsden, Eccles, Flixton, Gorton, Irlam & Cadishead, Levenshulme, Partington, Pendlebury, Pendleton, Prestwich, Stretford, Swinton, Urmston and Worsley. Other authorities obtaining water from Manchester, with which to

[1] Year of Drought.
[2] Additional quantity of water from Thirlmere was first delivered at Manchester by the second pipe on Nov. 3rd 1904.

supply some of the townships within their area of supply, are the Stockport Corporation, the North Cheshire Water Company and the Hyde Corporation. Supplies of water are also given from the Thirlmere Aqueduct to the Wigan Corporation, the District Councils of South Westmorland, Lunesdale, Walton-le-Dale, Chorley, Preston, Lancaster, Tyldesley and Atherton and the Carnforth Waterworks Company. The estimated population supplied is about 1 200 000.

Water is sold partly at an annual charge, based upon the rent of the property, and partly according to the quantity consumed, measured by a meter. Where the corporation provides a supply in detail beyond the city limits, a higher charge is made than for a corresponding supply within the city limits. The following are the charges within the City: public water rate, threepence in the pound, upon the poor rate assessment[1] on all property, payable by the owner. Domestic water rate, ninepence in the pound, upon the poor rate assessment on all dwelling houses. No dwelling house is charged less than 5 s per annum, if internally, or 4 s, if externally, supplied with water. The domestic water rate on houses assessed at £ 10 and under, and on all houses assessed above that amount, the rent of which is payable at any shorter period than three months, is charged to the owner, who is allowed a discount of 20 per cent, provided he owns at least three houses within the area and pays the rate on or before the 31st October, whether the said houses be occupied or unoccupied[2].

Beyond the limits of the City, dwelling houses pay 1 s in the £ on the net annual value, no house being charged less than 8 s per annum. The water rate on houses, the rent of which is payable at any shorter period than three months, is charged to the owner, who is allowed a discount of 20 per cent, provided there are not fewer than three in number and payment is made on or before the 31st August, whether the same be occupied or unoccupied.

Baths in weekly houses, within and beyond the limits of the City, are charged 5 s each per annum, in addition to the supply for domestic purposes, a discount of 20 per cent being allowed, if paid for in advance. Extra charges are also made for tubes

---

[1] This is normally five-sixths of the annual rental.
[2] The financial year of the Waterworks Department begins on April 1st.

for watering gardens and greenhouses and for washing windows or flags.

In cases where there is a doubtful consumption of water, a meter is fixed. A quarterly charge is then made for the hire and maintenance of the meter, varying from 3 s to 35 s, according to the size of the pipe, and the water is paid for according to the amount consumed, subject to a minimum quarterly charge. Below a few examples are given from the scales of charges per quarter.

Quantity of water in Galls.	Charge within the City			Charge outside the City			Quantity of water in Galls.	Charge within the City			Charge outside the City		
	£	s	d	£	s	d		£	s	d	£	s	d
1 000	—	2	—	—	2	—	1 500 000	39	11	8	39	11	8
10 000	—	18	8	—	18	8	1 722 000	43	1	1/2	43	1	1/2
100 000	6	9	--	6	9	—	above 1 722 000	—	—	—	6 d per 1000 gallons.		
250 000	12	8	9	12	8	9	2 000 000	47	5	3½	--	—	—
500 000	20	17	1	20	17	1	2 500 000	54	5	11	--	—	—
750 000	26	5	11¼	26	5	11¼	3 000 000	60	13	6	—	—	—
1 000 000	30	19	8½	30	19	8½	above 3 000 000	4,85 d per 1000 gallons.			—	—	—

The meter system of paying for water is generally used by factories, warehouses, shops and offices. It is also used where water is supplied for purposes of hydraulic pressure. Some years ago the Waterworks Committee laid down within the City a system of hydraulic power, 'capable of being utilised for working lifts, hoists, cranes, presses, suction cleaners, and other machinery. The pressure is 1000 lbs per square inch and the supply is continuous. On March 31st, 1909, power was being supplied to 2078 machines, contained in 539 premises, the total length of mains laid being 22 miles 1237 yards.

During the year ending March 31st, 1909, the City received the following sums from the sale of water.

(See table on page 24.)

Other receipts, including Meter Rents, House, Farm and Chief Rents, Bankers' and other interest, raised the total receipts to £ 407 609. After paying the working expenses of the Department, which consisted of £ 6150. 4. 1 chief and other rents, £ 39 950. 3. 11 Rates, Taxes and Tithes and £ 75 410. 12. 5 cost of maintenance and administration, there remained £ 286 097. 19. 8. This was devoted principally to the service of the debt of the Corporation in respect of waterworks, of which £ 5 735 139 was outstanding on March 31st, 1909. The interest charge for the year was £ 198 443 and the sum allotted to the sinking fund was £ 64 229, leaving a surplus of £ 23 983, which was available towards the reduction of the deficit of the Department.

Manchester Waterworks — Receipts from sale of Water.

	Within the City			Beyond the City.		
	£	s	d	£	s	d
Public water rate 1908—09	47 859	6	3	—	—	—
Domestic water rate 1908—09	54 537	5	7	—	—	—
	102 396	11	10			
Receipts for water supplied through Meters:						
Hydraulic Pressure	28 336	7	9	—	—	—
For Manufacturing Purposes	61 601	1	10	27 286	16	1
To Warehouses, Shops, Offices, etc.	34 329	1	7	3 802	6	10
Receipts for water supplied to Warehouses, Shops, Offices, etc. at fixed rentals	24 904	5	6	5 729	16	9
Receipts for water supplied for domestic purposes	—	—	—	54 745	1	11
Receipts for water supplied to Corporations, Local Authorities & Private Companies	—	—	—	54 400	15	—
	251 567	8	6	145 964	16	7

Total £ 397 532 5 s 1 d.

The total cost of the Waterworks was as follows:

Old Company's Works	£	533 561
Longdendale, etc.		2 850 426
Thirlmere		3 662 219
Hydraulic pressure		214 219
	£	7 260 425

The total sum borrowed in connection with the Waterworks has been £ 7 462 579, of which £ 1 727 440 has been paid off by means of the sinking fund, leaving an outstanding debt of nearly five and three quarter million pounds, as stated above.

Gas supply.

The Manchester Gas Works were established in 1817 by the Police Commissioners, who were at that time the Governing Body of the town. On the 24th June, 1843, the powers and duties of the Commissioners were transferred to the Corporation, and from that date the Gas Works became municipal property. A few small plants were built outside Manchester, when the City did not cover such a large area as at present, but when the City had extended its mains, so that it could reach the areas supplied by these Companies, they were taken over by Manchester. The two most important cases were the purchase of the Provincial Portable Gas Company in Hulme in 1857 and of the Droylsden Gas Company in 1869.

The undertaking, as it exists to-day, comprises four works in different parts of the City.

The Gaythorn Works occupy a site of 8 acres 4487 sq. yards, the land, buildings and apparatus being valued in the books on March 31st, 1908, at £ 287 688. There are two retort houses, the one capable of producing 1 500 000 cubic feet of gas daily and the other 2 250 000 cubic feet of gas daily. At the present time, new retorts are being erected which will double the productive capacity of the second retort house. There are seven gasholders at the works with a total capacity of 6 010 000 cubic feet.

The Rochdale Road Works occupy a site of 9 acres 339 sq. yards, the land, buildings and apparatus being valued at £ 332 004 on March 31, 1908. There are three retort houses with a total manufacturing capacity of 6 000 000 cubic feet per day. There are five gasholders with a total capacity of 4 100 000 cubic feet.

The Bradford Road Works are the newest and the largest of the four works. The land, 52 acres 3856 sq. yards, was acquired in 1870, the foundation stone was laid in 1877 and gas was first manufactured in 1884. The total value of the works on March 31, 1908, including land, buildings and apparatus, was £ 807 967. There are two retort houses with a total manufacturing capacity of 8 000 000 cubic feet per day. There are five gasholders with a total storage capacity of 13 800 000 c. ft., the largest, with a diameter of 250 feet, alone holding 7 000 000 cubic feet. An even larger gasholder, with a diameter of 282 feet, is under construction.

Another installation at the Bradford Road Works is the Carburetted Water Gas Plant, consisting of eight sets of Humphrey & Glasgow's producing apparatus of a total capacity of 6 500 000 cubic feet per diem.

At this station an experimental gas works has been erected, complete in every detail from retorts to governor. The capacity of the works is 60 000 cubic feet per diem. The plant is used for the testing of coal and general research work in the methods of manufacture, as a guide to the working of the various stations.

A plant of the capacity of 40 tons per day, in two sets, for the conversion of the ammoniacal liquor, produced at the various works, into sulphate of ammonia, has been erected at Bradford Road, also a plant of a capacity of 80 tons a week for the manufacture of sulphuric acid from spent oxide or pyrites.

The Droylsden Works are quite small (area of site, 4 acres 3789 sq. yards) and were acquired by the Corporation from the Droylsden Gas Company in 1869. The book value on March 31st, 1908, was £ 26 269. There is one retort house with a daily manufacturing capacity of 400 000 cubic feet, whilst there are two gasholders with a total storage capacity of 600 000 cubic feet.

To summarise the results, the total manufacturing capacity of all the works in 24 hours is

	Cubic feet
Coal Gas	18 150 000,
Carburetted Water Gas	6 500 000.
Total	24 650 000.

The total storage capacity of all gasholders is 24 510 000 cubic feet. The gas is distributed by means of 912$^1/_2$ miles of main pipes, varying in diameter from 36 inches to two inches. The mains are cast iron, with turned and bored joints and are in many cases substantially laid on concrete. It is a somewhat costly method, but the small percentage of gas unaccounted for justifies the expenditure. Of the total quantity of gas sent out in 1907—1908, 96,48 per cent was accounted for, the loss by leakage and condensation being only 3,52 per cent.

Independent mains have been laid connecting the Gaythorn, Rochdale Road and Bradford Road Works respectively, and gas can be transmitted directly from one works to another without difficulty.

On March 31, 1908, there were 148 652 consumers within the city and 22 286 consumers without the city, which gives a total of 170 938 consumers; the outside townships supplied from the Corporation mains being the following: Audenshaw, Cheadle, Droylsden, Failsworth, Gorton, Levenshulme, Northenden, Northen Etchells, Stockport Etchells and part of Stretford. The consumers within and beyond the city boundary may be classified, according to the type of meter used, as follows:

	By ordinary Meter	By prepayment Meter	Total
Within the City . . .	98 249	50 403	148 652
Without the City . .	16 321	5 963	22 286
Total	114 570	56 368	170 938

The automatic, prepayment, or penny-in-the-slot meters are very popular amongst the working classes. They were first introduced in January, 1891, when 25 cubic feet of gas were supplied for a penny. In September, 1898, the quantity supplied for a penny was increased to 30 cubic feet. The amount of cash collected therefrom during the year 1907—1908 was £ 72 737, or an average from each meter of £ 1. 5. 9. The average annual consumption by these meters was 9309 cubic feet within the city and 8215 cubic feet without the city.

In 1907—1908 the output of gas from the four works was 5777 million cubic feet; the quantity of gas sold being 4922 million cubic feet within the city and 524 million cubic feet without the city, the percentage of consumption being 90.4 within the city and 9.6 without the city. These figures include not only the consumption of gas by ordinary and by automatic consumers for lighting and heating purposes, but the gas consumed in gas engines, gas stoves and public lamps. Details concerning the distribution of gas are given below:

	Within the City	Without the City	Total
Ordinary Consumers:			
Number	98 249	16 321	114 570
Gas Consumed cu. ft.	3 236 264 000	330 904 000	3 567 168 000
Proportion of total gas sold .	59,42 %	6,08 %	65,50 %
Automatic Consumers:			
Number	50 403	5 965	56 368
Gas Consumed cu. ft.	469 068 000	49 000 000	518 068 000
Proportion of total gas sold .	8,61 %	0,90 %	9,51 %
Gas Engines:			
Number	1604	137	1741
Gas Consumed cu. ft.	395 671 000	30 459 000	426 130 000
Proportion of total gas sold .	7,26 %	0,56 %	7,82 %
Gas Stoves:			
Number	35 076	6 380	41 456
Gas Consumed cu. ft.	482 275 000	87 725 000	570 000 000
Proportion of total gas sold .	8,86 %	1,61 %	10,47 %
Public Lamps:			
Number	18 478	2 285	20 763
Gas Consumed cu. ft.	339 100 000	25 817 000	364 917 000
Proportion of total gas sold .	6,23 %	0,47 %	6,70 %
Total sold cu. ft.	4 922 378 000	523 905 000	5 446 283 000
Proportion of total gas sold .	90,38 %	9,62 %	100 %

The use of gas for cooking is becoming more and more common, due, to some extent at least, to the fact that since June 24, 1903, the Corporation makes no charge for the hire of stoves. On March 31st, 1905, there were 23 862 gas cookers owned and fixed by the city. A year later there were 29 760 stoves and in addition 26 186 grillers in connection with automatic and small ordinary meters. About 35 per cent of the gas consumers had free use of a cooker or griller. On March 31, 1907, there were 36 214 stoves and 28 452 grillers in use, some 39 per cent of the consumers having free use of one or the other. On March 31, 1908, the figures for cookers and grillers had risen to 41 456 and 29 706 respectively, which were used by some 41 per cent of the consumers.

No reduction is made in the charge for gas used for cooking or heating purposes. On the other hand, where gas is supplied for power, a somewhat lower tariff is in force. The number of gas engines in use has remained fairly constant the last few years. On March 31, 1905, there were 1711 gas engines in use, whilst the quantity of gas consumed by these engines during the previous year was 386 982 000 cubic feet. The corresponding figures for 1906 were 1775 engines and 414 089 000 cubic feet of gas; for 1907 1732 engines and 416 227 000 cubic feet of gas, and for 1908 1741 engines and 426 130 000 cubic feet of gas. The horse power of these 1741 engines was 11 397.

Having described the works and the distribution of gas, we may now turn to the manufacturing processes. During the year 1907—1908 the following materials were used at the works:

Coal . . . . 405 279 tons,
Cannel . . . . 16 086 tons,
Oil (2 709 355 gallons) }
Benzol (52 945 gallons) } . . 106 526 tons.
----
527 891 tons.

The total quantity of coal gas produced was 4 615 139 000 cubic feet, or 10 948 cubic feet per ton of coal used. The total quantity of coke produced was 283 408 tons, or 13,45 cwt, per ton of coal carbonized. Of the total quantity of coke produced, 65 412 tons or 23,08 per cent were used in the works, so that the quantity available for sale, including 28 639 tons used in the manufacture of carburetted water gas and sulphate of ammonia, was 217 996 tons, or 10,35 cwts. per ton carbonized. The quantity of coal tar produced was 25 905 tons, or 11,75 gallons per ton of coal carbonized. The quantity of ammoniacal liquor produced of 10 oz strength, was 11 615 608 gallons, or 27,57 gallons per ton of coal carbonized. From the ammoniacal liquor, 4429 tons of sulphate of ammonia were made.

During the year 1 164 117 000 cubic feet of carburetted water gas were produced. This represents 20,14 per cent of the total output of gas. To produce this water gas, 2 709 355 gallons of oil and 23 990 tons of coke were used. The quantity of carburetted water gas tar produced was 2515 tons, or 50,06 gallons per ton of oil used.

On the following page a table is given showing the financial aspect of the manufacture and distribution of gas for year 1907—1908. The actual amounts of the various charges are given and also the cost per 1000 cubic feet sold, which enables the reader to realize immediately, how much of the price obtained for every 1000 cubic feet is required to meet the various classes of expenditure.

Manchester Corporation Gas Works — Expenditure Account — For Year Ending 31. 3. 08.

	Amount	Per 1000 cub. ft. sold.
Manufacture:	£	d
Coal	299 511	13,20
Less Residuals	160 134	7,06
Net cost of coal	139 377	6,14
Coke and Water (carburetted water gas)	8 554	0,38
Salaries	6 187	0,27
Carbonizing wages	47 618	2,10
Purification	1 056	0,04
Wear & Tear	52 664	2,32
Renewals of Plant	19 734	0.87
Net cost of gas in holder	275 190	12,12
Distribution:		
Salaries & Wages	25 437	1,12
Repairs, etc., Mains, Meters & Stoves	32 826	1,45
Renewal of Mains etc.	44 365	1,95
Total Distribution	102 628	4,52
Rents, Rates & Taxes	55 590	2,45
Management:		
Salaries & Wages	4 900	0,21
Cost of Collection	11 924	0,53
General Charges	7 466	0,33
Bad Debts	870	0.04
Total management	25 160	1.11
	458 568	20.20
Less rents, etc.	865	0,04
Net cost of gas delivered	457 703	20,16
Capital Charges (interest and sinking fund)	106 379	4,69
Real cost of gas delivered	563 082	24,85

At the present time there are six different prices of gas, namely:

By ordinary meter for general purposes:
Within the city . . . . 2 s 3 d per 1000 cubic feet.
Without the city . . . . 2 s 6 d „ 1000 „ „

By ordinary meter for power purposes:
Within the city . . . . . 1 s 9 d per 1000 cubic feet.
Without the city. . . . . 2 s 0 d „ 1000 „ „
By automatic meter:
Within the city, 30 ft, for 1 d = 2 s 9 d per 1000 cubic feet.
Without the city, 25 ft, „ 1 d = 3 s 4 d „ 1000 „ „

No charge is made for the hire of meters or stoves.

There are no statutory provisions regarding the character or quality of the service, and the illuminating power has been reduced of recent years, since the use of incandesant mantles has become so common. In 1889, the illuminating power of the gas sent from the works, as tested by the Metropolitan No. 2 burner, was equivalent to 20,14 sperm candles, and during the next ten years it was always above 19, but in 1908 it was equivalent to only 17,53 standard sperm candles, and in one or two of the previous years it had been even lower.

The total borrowing powers of the Manchester Corporation in respect of the Gas Works, under various acts since the undertaking was transferred to the Corporation, amount to £ 2 700 640. The total sum raised by loans is £ 2 451 650, but of this more than half has been repaid by means of the sinking fund, so that the present loan debt of the undertaking is only £ 1 216 039. The exact financial position of the Department may be best seen from the general Balance Sheet given below.

(See table on next page.)

The question of the sale of residuals and the policy pursued by the Gas Committee with regard to the price of gas and the profits of the undertaking will be discussed later in other sections. Here it may be noted that the number of employees, including 397 members of the administrative staff, was 2083 on March 31, 1908.

Electricity Supply.

The electricity undertaking in Manchester has been a municipal enterprise ever since current has been supplied in the city, which was first done in July, 1893. Originally the undertaking was managed by the Gas Committee, but since 1897 there has been a separate Electricity Committee.

Manchester Corporation Gas Works — General Balance Sheet:

Liabilities	31st March 1908.		Assets	
Loan Debts	₤ 1 216 039	Land, Buildings, Plant etc.	₤ 2 700 699	
Sundry Creditors . .	151 077	Stocks on Hand . . .	113 540	
Bankers	9 179	Treasurer.	764	
Total Liabilities	₤ 1 376 295	Sundry Debtors . . .	178 511	
Surplus and sinking Fund	1 396 695			
Profits applied to extension of works where borrowing powers are not granted:				
Carburetted Water Gas Plant . . .	85 462			
Whitworth St. West Depot	15 574			
Chemical Works. .	9 137			
General Extensions	23 319			
Renewals Account. .	44 190			
Reserve Fund Account	42 881			
	₤ 2 993 514		₤ 2 993 514	

There are three main electric generating stations in Manchester, two directly in the heart of the city, the Bloom Street Station and the Dickinson Street Station, and one about three miles from the commercial centre, the Stuart Street Station. In addition there are twenty-two sub-stations, three of which are beyond the city boundary, which are equipped with motor driven generators and balancers. The sub-stations are scattered all over the city and outlying districts, their principal output being for the tramways service.

The Dickinson Street Generating Station occupies a site of 5 798 square yards. Its electrical equipment consists of one dynamo of 1500 kilowatts, four generators of 750 kilowatts each, one of 1500 and two of 1800, giving a total capacity of 9 600 kilowatts. The capacity of the steam engines installed at the Dickinson Street Station is 15 800 horse power.

The Bloom Street Generating Station is the smallest of the three. It occupies only 1923 square yards. Its electrical equipment consists of four generators of 1800 kilowatts each, driven by steam engines of 14 000 horse power capacity. The system and pressure in the Dickinson Street and Bloom Street Area is direct-current low-pressure: for lighting, 100 volts and 200 volts, the former in the centre of the city, on the old five-wire system; new supplies being connected at the higher pressure. For power, 200 volts for motors up to $3^1/_2$ horse power and 400 volts for motors over $3^1/_2$ horse power. For traction, 500 volts, and for street lighting 100, 200, 300 and 400 volts.

The Stuart Street Generating Station is by far the largest, the site being 60 608 square yards. Its electrical equipment consists of nine generators, six of 1500 kilowatts each, two of 3750 kilowatts each and one of 6000 kilowatts, giving a total capacity of 22 500 kilowatts. The capacity of the steam engines at the station is 37 000 HP. The system and pressure of the Stuart Street Area is alternating-current high-pressure transformed and converted at sub-stations to direct-current low-pressure. Current is supplied at 200 volts for lighting purposes, at 200 and 400 volts for ordinary power purposes and at 500 volts for traction. In special cases, large consumers of current for power purposes are supplied with alternating high-pressure current, which is transformed on their own premises to the required pressure.

The total normal capacity of the plant at the end of each financial year and the maximum loads on the plant during the same period, give a good indication of the growth of the undertaking.

31st March	(1) Normal Capacity of Plant	(2) Maximum Load	(3) Ratio of (2) to (1) in percentages:
	KW	KW	
1894	1 360	651	47,9
1895	1 860	1 187	63,9
1896	3 240	2 082	64,3
1897	3 600	2 737	76,0
1898	3 360	3 776	—
1899	4 860	4 246	87,4
1900	5 880	5 607	95,4
1901	7 140	6 876	96,3
1902	14 450	9 140	63,3
1903	23 050	12 775	55,4
1904	26 050	17 290	66,4
1905	25 300	20 023	79,1
1906	32 800	21 928	66,9
1907	33 800	25 180	74,5
1908	39 300	27 709	70,5
1909	39 300	31 118	79,2

Another means of indicating the steady growth of the Electricity Department during the sixteen years it has existed, is to take the figures showing the lamp and motor connections at the end of each financial year.

Year ending March 31st	Number of Consumers	Number of Motors	Total Lamp and Motor connections in 8 C.P.
1894	412	11	41 143
1895	738	13	66 820
1896	1148	47	103 266
1897	1581	122	143 398
1898	1981	214	183 408
1899	2590	343	247 457
1900	3228	497	319 286
1901	3788	672	383 466
1902	4013	774	414 115
1903	4541	1025	475 541
1904	5171	1460	607 451
1905	5729	1917	735 382
1906	6340	2320	848 087
1907	6989	2805	1 035 221
1908	7519	3295	1 238 739
1909	8125	3762	1 469 519

The total quantity of electricity generated during the year 1908—1909 was 88 766 232 Board of Trade units [1]. The quantity used in the works was 6 791 020 units, whilst the quantity sold was 66 924 864 units. The balance, 15 050 348 units, which was the quantity used in distribution, or otherwise not accounted for, represents 16,96 % of the quantity issued from the generating stations. The cost of producing the electricity generated in 1908—1909 was £ 184 039, or including the sums set aside for renewals, interest and sinking fund, £ 355 241, which may be analysed as follows.

(See table page 35.)

The figures in this table are the average costs of low-pressure and high-pressure supplies furnished under widely varying conditions as to load and diversity factors. Consequently they afford no guide to the cost of individual supplies.

---

[1] A Board of Trade Unit is the same as a Kilowatt hour, that is, the consumption of 16 ordinary 16 candle power glow lamps for an hour.

Analysis of Expenditure of Electricity Department on Revenue Account, during the year ending March 31, 1909.

	Total cost	Average cost per Unit sold
	£	d
Coal, etc.	67 219	0,24
Oil, waste, water and engine room stores	6 926	0,02
Wages and Salaries	33 622	0,12
Repairs and Maintenance of Buildings, Plant. etc.	30 114	0,11
	137 881	0,49
Rents, Rates and Taxes	32 461	0,12
Management Expenses etc.	13 697	0,05
	184 039	0,66
Interest and Sinking Fund	149 707	0,53
Renewals suspense	21 495	0,08
Totals	355 241	1,27

The Manchester Corporation supplies consumers not only in the city, but also in certain adjacent districts, namely, Levenshulme, Droylsden, Heaton Norris, Audenshaw, Denton, Failsworth and Gorton. In each case the Manchester Corporation has taken over the Lighting Order for a period of 21 years, at the end of which the various authorities may, when due notice has been given, take over such of the undertaking as lies within their districts. The oldest of these agreements, that with Levenshulme, expires in 1918. Three expire in 1920, one in 1922, one in 1923 and the last in 1926. With regard to the rates of charge, no difference is made between consumers within and without the city, as is the case with gas. On the other hand, a very considerable difference is made between the charge for lighting and the charge for power.

The scale of charges at present in force is given below:

Lighting: a) $3^3/_4$ d per unit metered, with a minimum charge of 30/— per annum, or, at the option of the consumer, b) $1^1/_2$ d per unit metered, plus a fixed charge of £ 7 per annum per kilowatt of demand (= 2 s 4 d per ordinary 16 candle power lamp per quarter).

Power (Motors and Radiators):

a) 1¼ d per unit for units below 300 per horse power per quarter year, with a minimum charge of 7/6 d per quarter year.
b) 1 d per unit for units amounting to 300 or more per horse power per quarter year.
c) 0,9 d per unit for units amounting to 400 or more per horse power per quarter year.
d) 0,8 d per unit for units amounting to 500 or more per horse power per quarter year.
e) 0,7 d per unit for units amounting to 600 or more per horse power per quarter year.

Alternatively, at the option of the consumer, 25 s per horse power demanded per quarter, plus ⅛ d per unit metered.

Power (Hoist): graduating scale from 1⅞ d to 1 d per unit.

The total borrowing powers of the Manchester Corporation in respect of the Electricity undertaking amount to £ 2 724 754 — the total loans raised since the commencement of the undertaking being £ 2 487 089. Of this amount a little over one fifth has been redeemed by means of the sinking fund. The present financial position of the Department can best be seen from the general Balance Sheet given below.

Manchester Corporation Electricity Works — General Balance Sheet:

Liabilities		31st March 1909	Assets	
Loan Debts	£ 1 957 589	Land, Buildings, Plant etc.	£ 2 568 993
Sundry Creditors	68 947	Stocks on hand	56 011
Total Liabilities	£ 2 026 536	Bankers	31 075
		Treasurer	3 546
Surplus and Sinking Fund	529 499	Reserve fund investment account	6 358
Profits applied to extension of works where borrowing powers are not granted	58 666	Sundry Debtors	90 328
Renewals suspense A/c	135 252		
Reserve Fund	6 358		
	£ 2 756 311		£ 2 756 311

The question of profits and selling policy is discussed elsewhere; here it may be noted, however, that the revenue of the department in 1908—1909 was £ 367 240, of which £ 231 648 was derived from the sale of current for lighting and power, £ 128 613 from the sale of current for traction purposes, and £ 855 from the sale of current for public lighting; of the total quantity of current sold, 37 249 615 Board of Trade units were sold for lighting, power and public lighting and 29 675 249 units for traction purposes.

Tramways Department.

Of all the large trading departments of the corporation, that of the Tramways is of the most recent origin. From 1877 until June, 1901, there was municipal ownership of the tracks and company operation of the service, and it was not until June, 1903, that the entire system was worked by the city. The nature of the agreement between the city and the company, and the history of the movement in favor of municipal management, are dealt with in later sections of this article. Here the object is to give a description of the Tramways system as it exists to-day.

The Manchester Corporation Tramways are entirely electric, equipped on the overhead system. The usual arrangement is for the wires to be spanned from standards fixed at the side of the roads, but in certain streets the wires are spanned from buildings, and in other cases centre poles or side poles with brackets are used.

The track is laid with the standard railway guage of 4 feet $8^{1}/_{2}$ inches. The rails weigh 103 lbs per yard and are usually 60 feet long. The height of the rail is 7 inches and the width of the base of the rail is also 7 inches. The roadway between the rails and tracks, and for a distance of 18 inches outside the outer rails, is paved at the cost of the tramway undertaking. Ordinarily granite setts are used, but in the centre of the town there is a good deal of wood pavement. The aggregate length of single track open for traffic on the 31st March, 1908, including the lines over which the Corporation was exercising running powers, was 176 miles, 1337 yards, composed as follows:

(See table on next page.)

The lines which are leased are all outside the city boundary, as well as those over which the Corporation is exercising running powers. These latter lines are situated in the boroughs of Ashton-

	Double Track		Single Track		Route Mileage		Aggregate Single Track	
	Mls.	Yds.	Mls.	Yds.	Mls.	Yds.	Mls.	Yds.
Owned	47	1455	19	765	67	460	115	155
Leased	21	727	4	306	25	1033	47	—
Lines over which Corporation is exercising running powers . .	5	1543	2	1616	8	1399	14	1182
Totals	75	205	26	927	101	1132	176	1337

under-Lyne and Oldham, whilst the former are in the boroughs of Stockport and Middleton and the Urban Districts of Altrincham, Dunham Massey, Ashton-on-Mersey, Sale, Stretford, Failsworth, Droylsden, Audenshaw, Gorton, Denton, Levenshulme and Heaton Norris. The line extending furthest beyond the city boundary is that to Altrincham, some eight miles of which lie outside the city area. This route, and that running to Waterhead, in the upper part of Oldham, are the longest on which through cars are run from the centre of the city, each being about nine miles long. The leases are of 21 years duration, and as a rule the Manchester Corporation has provided the electrical equipment to operate the lines on the overhead system, and at the end of the lease must remove this equipment, unless the local authorities purchase it by agreement or arbitration.

The Tramways Department has no generating plant of its own, but purchases all energy required from the Municipal Electricity Department, except for the leased lines in Middleton, Ashton-under-Lyne, Stockport and Stretford. In each of these cases, the local electricity station supplies the energy for the section of the line in its respective district. The arrangement between the Tramways and the Electricity Departments, regarding the charges made to the former for energy used, is as follows:

1. A fixed annual charge per kilowatt installed to meet the maximum demand for traction purposes, with the addition of

2. A charge of so much per unit supplied to cover the running expenses.

The fixed annual charge per kilowatt is made up of three items:

a) interest and sinking fund in respect of moneys borrowed by the Electricity Committee for the provision of land and buildings for a generating station, boilers, engines, generators, high pressure switching gear, high pressure mains, transforming plant, land and buildings for transforming stations and low pressure feeders up to the trolley wires;

b) the provision of a sum to be set aside each year as a renewals fund, it being understood that the amount so set aside shall be subject to the approval of the Tramways Committee;

c) a proper proportion of the cost of coal and wages.

The charge per unit supplied is to be the actual cost of generating the current with the addition thereto of 3 per cent profit.

In 1907—1908, the price paid by the Tramways Department to the Electricity Department for energy was 1,14 d per unit. The following year the price had fallen to 1,04 d per unit.

On March 31, 1908, the stock of cars belonging to the Manchester Corporation was 566. The great majority of the cars are double-deckers, with sitting accommodation inside and outside. There are two different sizes, the larger, mounted on double trucks, has accommodation for 80, the smaller, mounted on a single truck, has accommodation for 50. The tops of many of the cars are covered, which is a distinct advantage in winter and in wet weather at all times, but the covered cars are not so agreeable as open cars in warm weather. In addition to the double-deck cars, there are a certain number of single-deck combination cars, used on routes which pass under low railway bridges. They have sitting accommodation both inside and on the platforms, and altogether carry 40 passengers. The exact number of cars in stock on March 31st, 1908, was as follows:

Type	Without Covered Tops.	With Covered Tops.	Total.
Single truck	194	115	309
Double truck	87	125	212
Combination	—	—	45
	281	240	566

There are three car-sheds, each with accommodation for some 250 cars, viz. Hyde Road Car Shed, Queen's Road Car Shed, and Princess Road Car-Shed. Works for building car-bodies and tops, and for carrying out repairs, have been erected at Hyde Road, adjoining the car-shed.

The fares charged on the Corporation Tramways vary from a halfpenny to fivepence halfpenny. The halfpenny fare has been adopted on the circular and cross routes only, not on the main routes radiating out from the centre of Manchester. There are no transfers of any kind. The most usual fare is a penny, as is clearly shown in the table given below.

Table Showing the Number and Percentage of Passengers Carried at various fares during the year 1907—08:

Fare	Number of Passengers Carried	Percentage
d		
$1/2$	10 487 467	6,92
1	102 739 872	67,82
$1^{1}/_{2}$	19 397 156	12,80
2	10 965 292	7,24
$2^{1}/_{2}$	3 187 535	2,10
3	2 723 300	1,80
$3^{1}/_{2}$	1 052 204	0,70
4	540 971	0,36
$4^{1}/_{2}$	146 292	0,10
5	75 764	0,05
$5^{1}/_{2}$	161 285	0,11
Total	151 477 138	100,00

Children under five, not occupying a seat, are carried free, whilst children under 12 pay half fares, but not less than a penny on a main route.

Workpeople travel at specially reduced fares. Any one travelling before seven o'clock in the morning can buy a ticket enabling him to travel nearly twice the usual distance for the ordinary fare. At the same time he can buy a return ticket available for the journey back in the evening. After seven o'clock, no workpeoples' tickets of any kind are issued and only those holding return tickets can travel home at reduced fares in the evening.

Whereas a penny was the most usual fare, the average fare paid per passenger in 1907—1908 was 1,21 d. The number of car miles was 16 974 955 and the average number of passengers per car mile was 8,92, whilst the average car miles per day per car was 98,5. The average traffic revenue per car mile was 10,76 d and the average traffic revenue per mile of single track was £ 4640.

The business of the Tramways Department is not entirely limited to carrying passengers; parcels are also carried to some extent. Shortly after the municipal system was in full working order, a somewhat ambitious parcel carrying scheme was organised. The ordinary trams formed only part of the basis of the scheme: special electrically equipped freight cars were built; a very considerable number of horses and vans were purchased; numerous hand carts were bought; some one hundred and fifty collecting and distributing depots were established and a large addition was made to the ordinary tramway staff. Parcels were collected and delivered anywhere within the cities of Manchester and Salford and part of Stretford at the following rates:

Up to 14 lbs weight 2 d.   Up to 56 lbs weight 4 d.
Up to 28 lbs weight 3 d.   Up to 112 lbs weight 6 d.

The rates outside of this area, and to and from any point in some 66 districts, including all the large towns except Bolton, and extending some 11 miles to the north, 8 miles to the east, 9 miles to the south, and 6 miles to the west, of the centre of Manchester were:

Up to 14 lbs weight 3 d.   Up to 56 lbs weight 6 d.
Up to 28 lbs weight 4 d.   Up to 112 lbs weight 8 d.

Breakable articles were carried at the ordinary rates, if at the risk of the owners, and at double these rates, if at the risk of the department.

This large scheme of parcel carrying was given up in October, 1906, as a big firm of general carriers took legal proceedings against the Tramways Committee, and the Courts held that the Department had considerably exceeded its legal powers. Furthermore, the system was worked at a heavy loss. A new system was begun on October 29th, 1906, which was limited to the area served by the Corporation Tramways, and to small parcels such as could be carried on the platforms of ordinary trams. A certain number of extra boys are engaged, who distribute parcels by means of bicycles and handcarts, but otherwise the trams constitute the basis of the system. A parcel can be handed to the conductor of any tram;

the charge made is 2 d or 3 d a parcel, according to weight and distance.

Analysis of Expenditure of the Tramways Department on Revenue Account, during the year ending March 31st, 1908.

	Total Cost	Average Cost Per Car Mile
	£	d
Traffic Expenses:		
Wages of Drivers and Guards	138 094	1,95
Wages of other traffic employees	21 880	0,31
Cleaning and Oiling Cars	22 060	0,31
Ticket Check	10 905	0,154
Miscellaneous	22 228	0,316
	215 217	3,04
General Repairs and Maintenance:		
Permanent way	13 599	0,19
Electrical equipment of line	7 535	0,106
Cars	46 798	0,66
Buildings, Plant, etc.	3 880	0,056
	71 812	1,012
Power Expenses:		
Cost of Current at 1,143 d per Board of Trade unit	142 879	2,02
General Expenses:		
Salaries, Rents, Rates, Compensation, Expenses of Legal Department, etc.	70 115	0,998
Total Working Expenses	500 023	7,07
Rent of leased lines	21 195	0,30
Interest on Capital	49 035	0,69
Sinking fund	41 748	0,59
Reserve, Renewals and Depreciation fund	87 790	1,24
Miscellaneous (Income Tax, Leaseholds, Expenses of 1907 Bill, Street Improvements)	16 385	0,23
	216 153	3,05
Total Expenditure	716 176	10,12

In what concerns the financial position of the Department, the total working expenses during the year 1907—1908 were just over £ 500 000, whilst other expenditure, including sums set aside for sinking fund, reserve, renewals and depreciation, brought the total outlay up to £ 716 000; in addition to this, the Department made a contribution of £ 55 000 towards the relief of the rates. The question of profits, however, as well as the fixing of fares, will be discussed in other sections of the article. Details of the expenditure will be found in the preceding table.

The total borrowing powers of the Manchester Corporation in respect of the Tramways undertaking amounted to £ 2 174 959 on March 31, 1908, whilst the total amount of loans raised since the commencement of the undertaking was £ 1 561 169. Of this amount a little over one tenth has been redeemed. The present financial position of the Department can be judged from the general balance sheet given below:

Manchester Corporation Tramways — General Balance Sheet.

Liabilities	March 31, 1908		Assets	
Loan Debts	£ 1 388 702	Permanent way	£	607 476
Sundry Creditors	44 547	Overhead equipment		174 705
Bankers	19 652	Car-sheds		295 510
Total Liabilities	£ 1 452 901	Rolling Stock		357 243
		Cost of Carriage Company's Undertaking		277 492
Sinking fund	182 627	Other Capital Expenditure		64 203
Loans Repayment Account	8 907			
		Total Outlay	£	1 776 629
Reserve, Renewals and Depreciation fund	382 977			
		Stocks on hand		91 610
		Sundry Debtors		120 833
		Cash in hand		16 586
		Miscellaneous		21 764
	£ 2 027 422		£	2 027 422

Some indication of the importance of the Department may be gathered from the fact that it employs 4500 men.

The Building and Letting of Houses.

Practically all municipal activity in this direction is based upon the Housing of the Working Classes Act, 1890, and subsequent amending acts. There are three different parts of the Act of 1890 under which the local authority may proceed: Part I provides for the clearing of large unhealthy areas in urban districts and the execution of an improvement scheme for the district dealt with; Part II relates to small areas; it provides for the closing and demolition of houses unfit for human habitation, for the removal of obstructive buildings and for the reconstruction of small areas condemned as unhealthy; under Part III the local authority can carry out a scheme to build houses for the working classes, without previously closing or demolishing insanitary property, or formally proving a deficiency of house accommodation. The town may buy the land compulsorily, if necessary, and either lease it to builders or others for the erection thereon of workmen's dwellings, or may itself undertake and carry out a building scheme. Under this part of the Act it appears feasible to acquire sites to be held for future needs.

The Corporation of Manchester has bought land under each part of the Act of 1890. In some cases, it has merely cleared a small slum area and made the site into an open space, but in other cases it has carried through a scheme of reconstruction.

The first unhealthy area to be dealt with, was that known as the Oldham Road area, which consisted of a number of properties and land about three quarters of a mile from the centre of the town. The site, which contained 18 269 square yards and on which 329 houses stood, was bought in 1891 for a total cost of £ 97 481. The houses were demolished, in consequence of which 1250 persons were displaced.

For purposes of rebuilding, the site was divided into two, known as Oldham Road Area, Block No. 1 and Oldham Road Area, Block No. 2. The latter has a superficial area of 7779 square yards. It has been covered by buildings five stories high, enclosing a large open quadrangle containing a superficial area of 4402 sq. yards. At each corner of the block, and facing Oldham Road, shops have been built with cellars underneath, the remainder of the ground floor and the four floors above being occupied by tenement dwellings. The dwellings on the upper floors are entered by balconies extending round all sides of the quadrangle, which are approached by stone staircases, leading immediately from the street entrances at each corner of the building. The tenements are arranged in pairs and consist principally of two rooms, namely, a living room containing about 174 sq. feet and 1566 cubic feet and a bedroom containing 108 sq. feet and 972 cubic feet. All the rooms are 9 feet high. Each tenement is provided with a well-ventilated food store and coal locker. Each pair of two-roomed tenements is entered from a common lobby, in which a water-closet and a sink are provided for the joint use of the occupants. At the four corners of the building, laundries and spacious drying rooms have been formed in the roof. Automatic gas meters are supplied to all the tenants.

The accommodation consists of 16 shops with cellars, let from £ 20 to £ 50 per annum; 237 two-roomed tenements, the weekly rent (including rates)[1] being 3/6 d to 5/— a week and 48 one-roomed tenements let for 2/6 d to 3/— per week. Double tenements are for families of two adults and one or two children: single tenements for one adult person or mother and child. The number of persons who can be accommodated is 848. The total cost of building the block, which was erected by contractors, was £ 60 577.

Oldham Road Area, No. 1 Block, contains a superficial area of 7498 sq. yards, on which have been erected four rows of buildings: 13 shops, with dwelling houses above, fronting Oldham Road, two rows of two story tenement buildings and eighteen five-roomed cottages. There are eight separate buildings in each of the two blocks of tenements. Each building contains four tenements, with a common entrance, the yards are common to four tenements, which have one, two or three rooms. The cottages have five rooms, a living room and a kitchen on the ground floor, two bedrooms on the first floor and an attic above. With regard to the accommodation, 11 of the shops, with five-room dwellings above, are let for £ 50 per annum; one for £ 60 per annum and one for £ 100 per annum. The rent of 16 one-room tenements is 3/— a week, of 32 two-room tenements 4/6 d a week, and of 16 three-room tenements 5/9 d per week. The 18 five-room cottages let for 7/9 d per week. In all, there is accommodation for 441 persons. The cost of the various buildings was £ 27 142. At the same time as the Oldham Road Area was being cleared, the Corporation acquired a property in Ancoats known as the Pollard Street Area, which consisted of 85 back-to-back houses and 14 shops, all old and worn out, the number of persons displaced being 396. The total cost was £ 9547. The site, afterwards built upon, had a superficial area of 3383 sq. yards. The buildings are very similar to those erected on the

---

[1] All the smaller weekly property is quoted inclusive of rates, unless expressly stated to the contrary.

Oldham Road Area, No. 2 Block, except that there are no shops. The buildings contain 130 two-room tenements, the rent of which is from 3/— to 4/— per week, and five one-room tenements, the weekly rent of which is 2/6 d. The total number of persons who can be accommodated is 488. The cost of erecting the buildings was £ 26 220.

The Oldham Road and Pollard Street Areas were all acquired under Part I of the Housing of the Working Classes Act of 1890. Three Areas to be acquired under Part II of the Act were those in Chester Street, Pott Street and Harrison Street. The Chester Street Area is situated in Hulme, and was purchased by the Corporation at a total cost of £ 15 141. The number of houses demolished was 133, which displaced 368 persons. The site of 4554 square yards has been utilized for the erection of four rows of tenement buildings, two stories high. Each building has a frontage of about 40 feet and contains two two-roomed and two three-roomed tenements, which have one common entrance and staircase. Altogether there are 36 two-room tenements, the weekly rent of which is 4/6 d, 18 three-room tenements let at 5/9 d per week and 18 three-room tenements let at 6/— per week. The 72 tenements accommodate 324 persons and cost £ 14 598 to build.

The Pott Street Area lies nearly midway between the Oldham Road and Pollard Street Areas. One hundred and twenty seven houses, tenanted by 399 persons, were purchased for £ 14 621 and demolished. A site of 3914 sq. yards was available for building purposes, and two rows of tenement dwellings, three stories high, were erected upon it. A common entrance and staircase provide access to three two-roomed and three three-roomed tenements. Two corner plots, which were unsuitable for dwellings, were utilized for the erection of shops, with warehouses above each shop, and a doorway leading into the adjoining tenement. The shops are rented for £ 25 and £ 35 per annum. Twelve two-room tenements let for 4/6 d a week and twenty-four for 4/3 d a week; 12 three-room tenements are rented for 5/6 d a week; 13 for 6/3 per week and 13 more for 5/— per week; one four-room tenement is let at 6/3 d per week and two others at 6/—; altogether there is accommodation for 316 persons, provided at a cost of £ 17 942.

The Harrison Street Area lies in Ancoats, one of the most congested working class districts in the City. Some 250 persons were displaced by the demolition of 79 houses and a site of 3375 sq. yards was available for building purposes at a cost of £ 5147. Here the Corporation decided to erect a lodging house for men. The building is three stories high and has a frontage of 178 feet and a depth of 118$^{1}/_{2}$ ft. In the basement there are lavatories, wash-house, foot-baths, ordinary baths, lockers for bundles, and a boot-cleaning room for lodgers. On the ground floor there are a large smoke-room, a dining-room and a reading-room, also kitchen, scullery and shop. On the ground floor, there are also dormitories containing 49 cubicles. The first and second floors are entirely set apart for sleeping accommodation. Each contains 157 cubicles, 5 feet wide and 7$^{1}/_{4}$ feet long, with a separate window opening direct into the air. Altogether the lodging house has accommodation for 363 men. The charge made is 6 d a night or 3/— a week. The cost of erecting the building was £ 23 564.

The most important scheme under Part III of the Housing of the Working Classes Act, 1890, is that connected with the Blackley Estate. This estate was purchased by the Corporation in 1900, for the purpose of providing houses for the working classes displaced by improvement schemes, and for satisfying the requirements of the government in respect to schemes carried out by the Education Committee. The estate, which is situated on the City boundary, about 4 miles from the centre of the city, consists of 243$^{1}/_{2}$ acres and was acquired at a cost of £ 36 646. Up to now, only a small area has been used for building purposes and allotment gardens, and most is leased to farmers. The number of cottages which have been erected is 150. Some have four rooms and others five rooms, whilst all have a bath, and small gardens back and front. The rents vary from 6/4 d to 7/— a week.

The most recent scheme to be carried out is that in Rochdale Road near the centre of the town, where a plot of land was purchased from the Improvement Committee for £ 1225 by the Sanitary Committee, who erected a block of tenements, comprising 32, consisting of two rooms, let at 4/6 d a week and 32, consisting of three rooms, let at 5/6 d per week. These tenements were first inhabited in 1906.

All the houses and tenements to which reference has been made so far, were erected by the Sanitary Committee, but there is one other Committee of the Corporation which have erected and own houses, viz: the Improvements Committee. This Committee erected 122 cottages at Miles Platting in fulfilment of statutory obligations in connection with street improvements. Sixty have four rooms and are let at 5/6 d per week and sixty-two have five rooms and are let at 7/— a week. The total cost of erecting the houses was £ 29 198, while the value of the land is £ 6836. There is an annual loss in connection with the houses, as in the case with those built by the Sanitary Committee, to which reference is made below. The deficit in 1907—1908, after paying cost of management, repairs, etc. and also all interest and sinking fund charges in respect of £ 36 000 borrowed, was £ 494 or 1,37 % on the capital outlay.

At the present time the Sanitary Committee have two sites in congested parts of the town on which the Corporation is to erect dwellings, but for the moment no progress is being made, as the committee are anxious to erect cottages, which would occasion a much more serious financial loss than would the erection of a block of tenement dwellings; in consequence of which the Town Council is not willing to approve of the scheme. The Corporation estate at Blackley is awaiting development, but for the present there seems no prospect of further building operations being undertaken.

Markets.

The institutions under the control of the Markets Committee belong to four different classes: a) markets proper; b) cold stores; c) slaughter houses; d) foreign animals wharf. The markets have belonged to the Corporation only since 1846, in which year the Corporation purchased the Manorial Rights and Properties from Sir Oswald Mosley, the Lord of the Manor, for £ 200 000, to be paid in annual instalments of £ 4000, the last payment being made in September, 1894. The Smithfield Markets are the centre of distribution for an area of about 50 miles, comprising a population of seven and a half millions. The fruit and vegetable market is the largest of its kind in the United Kingdom, whilst the fish market is surpassed only by the Billingsgate Market in London. There is a very important carcass market in connection with the city abattoirs, the number of carcasses exposed for sale, during the year 1907—1908, being as follows:

Manchester.

Beef	93 602
Mutton	357 953
Lamb	113 012
Veal	21 103
Pork	42 627
	528 297

There are two cold stores owned by the Corporation. The older, opened in 1895, is established in connection with the carcass market and abattoirs; and the newer, inaugurated in 1904, is erected under the retail fish market, for the convenience of tenants and others. The former is much larger than the latter, and cost some £ 80 000 to erect and equip, and has a storage capacity equal to 120 000 carcasses of mutton.

The City Abattoirs were opened in 1872 and have subsequently been extended in 1894 and again in 1902. Below are given figures showing the number of animals slaughtered during the year 1907—1908:

Beasts	33 914
Sheep	132 691
Lambs	44 533
Calves	2 142
Pigs	13 535
	226 815

The Foreign Animals Wharf has been built on land adjoining the Ship Canal for the landing and slaughter of animals from certain foreign countries. The site, containing some twelve acres, together with the buildings, cost nearly £ 100 000. Accommodation is provided for about 1850 head of cattle and 1200 sheep, with sufficient land for an extension up to 3000 head of cattle and 6000 sheep. During the year 1904—1905, 29 278 beasts, and 10 606 sheep were landed at the wharf, but since then the numbers have fallen somewhat.

Cleansing Department.

The Cleansing Committee are responsible for the sweeping and watering of the streets, roadways, passages and courts within the City, and for the collection and disposal of nightsoil and other refuse from dwellings, warehouses and public institutions, and also undertake the cleansing of the various markets, slaughter houses and abattoirs in the City. They employ about 1900 men and 450 horses, and for the purpose of their work require some 650 vehicles, including a large number of vans, carts and lurries, also a steam tug, a fleet of ten barges, about 172 heavy railway waggons, 4 small locomotives and 133 light railway trucks.

As far as practicable, the Committee do all their own work. They also excecute a considerable amount of work for other Committees. They build vans, lurries and carts, and keep in repair all the machinery and rolling stock used in the department, make harness, brushes, and receptacles for closets, refuse etc., and manufacture concentrated manure, mortar, soap, oils, grease and disinfecting powder.

Within the City, the Committee own 21 depots, together with tips at Harpurhey and Clayton Vale, comprising 82 acres; they also possess estates at Irlam, Chat Moss, and Carrington 3739 acres in extent.

In the City of Manchester there are 759 miles of streets, (exclusive of Withington). The principal streets are swept daily and the others once, twice or three times a week. The wood pavements and principal streets in the centre of the City are swilled periodically. There are 58 636 pail-closets and 94 739 ash-boxes and ash-bins, which require their contents removing once, twice or three times a week, whilst 7571 privies and middens are emptied as occasion demands. The excreta collected in the pails from the northern portion of the City are removed by vans to the Holt Town Depot where they are dried into portable manure, and readily disposed of to farmers at £ 3 per ton. The contents of the pails from the southern portion of the City are removed by vans to Water Street Depot where they are mixed with fine ashes from the riddlings of domestic refuse and dispatched by barge on the Manchester Ship Canal to the Carrington and Chat Moss Estates some eight miles from Manchester. The nightsoil from the middens is sold to farmers and utilized as manure for the land.

The dry combustible material received at Holt Town and Water Street Depots is consumed in Galloway boilers and generates steam for working the machinery, or is destroyed in destructor furnaces. The resulting clinker is ground into mortar and grit for the streets, or is sent away to the two estates to be utilized for roadmaking and ballasting of railway lines. The refuse and garbage removed from the market is destroyed in the destructor furnaces at the Water Street Depot. Seven thousand tons of slaughter-house and fish refuse is removed to the Holt Town Depot where it is dried up and added to the concentrated manure. Street sweepings are generally desposited in the nearest depot to drain and are afterwards carted to tips, or are sold to farmers as manure. The total quantity of refuse collected and disposed of by the Cleansing Department during the year 1907—1908 amounted to 336 511 tons.

Of the four principal depots, two have been mentioned: the Holt Town Depot where 99 287 tons of material were treated during 12 mounths and where 4646 tons of concentrated manure were manufactured and sold to farmers and others, the demand for this manure being greatly in excess of the supply. A considerable quantity of mortar was also produced and sold. The Water Street Works treated 155 160 tons of refuse from the southern side of the City, during the year ending March 31, 1908. Some was destroyed, some was shipped away and a certain amount of mortar was produced and sold. The Oldham Road Depot is used as a works for the manufacture and repair of the rolling stock of the department, and contains saw mills, timber sheds, brush making works, disinfecting ovens, ambulance-sheds and mortar-mills. The Caythorpe Street Depot, Moss Side, contains a destructor, mortar-mill and clinker-crusher. Large quantities of clinkers, both crushed and uncrushed, are disposed of to contractors and used in the construction of new streets. The mortar manufactured is disposed of at 4/— per ton. The fine dust removed from the flues is mixed with liquid carbolic acid and utilized as disinfecting powder. During the year 1907—1908, 15 310 tons of refuse were dealt with at this depot.

The Carrington Estate is situated about 10 miles from Manchester, in the parishes of Carrington and Dunham in the County of Cheshire. The estate was purchased by the Corporation in 1886, with the object of providing an outlet for the disposal of nightsoil and refuse, other than that dealt with within the confines of the City. The purchase price was £ 39 166 and since then an additional sum of £ 43 976 has been expended on capital account in the drainage of land, in the formation and equipment of a light railway, in farm and other buildings, roads, etc., making the total cost to March 31,

1909, ℒ 83142, whilst the City Surveyor's valuation of the estate three years previously was ℒ 108586. The repayment of the amount borrowed for the purchase of the estate extends over 50 years from 1886, and the amount for works is repayable in 30 years from the dates of borrowing which range from 1886 to 1891. The payments during the year 1908—1909 were ℒ 1337 for interest and ℒ 2222 to the sinking fund, a total of ℒ 3659.

At the time of purchase, the estate comprised 600 acres of wild moss, 209 acres of cultivated moss, 282 acres of agricultural land and 10 acres of roads etc., or a total of 1101 acres. Since the purchase of the estate the whole of the wild moss and the partially cultivated moss have been drained, delved, manured and brought into a thorough state of cultivation. The Parks and Cemeteries Committee of the Manchester Corporation have $58^1/_2$ acres of land as a nursery upon which they grow shrubs for the Manchester Parks. Nurserymen and market-gardeners occupy a considerable area, and grow shrubs and vegetables upon an extensive scale. The estate is now divided as fallows:

18 tenants occupy	1013	acres
Cottages, siding and wharf .	$11^3/_4$	,,
Roads and plantations . . .	$75^1/_2$	,,
Sand-hole	$3/_4$	,,
	1101	acres

The rents received from the estate for the 12 months ending 31 March, 1909, amounted to ℒ 2065.

During the year 1907—1908, 17106 tons of material were sent to the Carrington Estate, whilst during the 20 years ending March 31, 1908, 762589 tons of material had been sent, or an average of 38129 tons per annum. The equipment for handling the material consists of 11 miles of tramway, a steam crane, one small locomotive, manure trucks and other rolling stock, a railway siding on the Cheshire Lines Committee Railway and a wharf on the Ship Canal.

The Chat Moss Estate is situated in the Townships of Barton-on-Irwell and Irlam in the County of Lancashire; it has a frontage of about $1^1/_4$ miles to the Manchester Ship Canal and lies about seven miles from Manchester. The estate comprises 2580 acres and was purchased at a total cost of ℒ 139143 in 1895. In addition, ℒ 60217 have been spent for the works necessary for the development of the estate, for the building and repair of farmsteads, the construction of roads and drains, the provision of a wharf on the Ship Canal and the construction of some 13 miles of light railway for the conveyance of manure to the tenants. The repayment of the amount borrowed for the purchase extends over 50 years from 1896 and the amount for works is repayable in 30 years from the date of borrowing. During the year 1908—1909, £ 5287 were paid for interest and £ 3257 were set aside for a sinking fund, making a total outlay of £ 8544. Some 2278 acres are occupied by 46 tenants, whilst the remaining 302 acres consist of moss land, plantations, roads, wharf etc. The rents received from all sources upon the estate in 1908—1909 amounted to £ 5237.

Manure and refuse were first sent to the estate in December, 1898. Last year, 54531 tons of material were sent there and from December 14, 1898, till March 31, 1909, 609 743 tons of material were received at the estate as compared with the 778 942 tons received at Carrington during the 21 years ending March 31, 1909.

Sewage Works.

The sewage of Manchester is treated at three sewage works which are under the control of the Rivers Committee: the Davyhulme Works into which an area of 13666 acres drains; the Withington Works with a drainage area of 5816 acres, and the Moss Side Works with a drainage area of 421 acres. The Davyhulme Sewage Works and the land adjoining it, which has been purchased for future extensions, are situated on the southern banks of the Manchester Ship Canal in the Townships of Davyhulme, Flixton and Carrington. The works are organised for the bacterial treatment of the sewage. The sewage, as it reaches the works, passes through a system of screens and catch-pits designed to intercept coarser floating matter and heavy detritus. The flow is either passed through open septic tanks on to the half-acre bacteria beds or, after simple sedimentation, on to the storm beds. The sludge which settles, or which accumulates in the course of time in the septic tanks, flows by gravity, or is pushed by manual labour, into channels leading to two ejectors from which it is forced under air pressure into two storage tanks near the banks of the Ship Canal below Barton Locks. From these tanks it flows by gravity into the sludge steamer and is deposited at sea beyond the Mersey Bar. A portion of the sludge however is pressed and disposed of among the neighbouring farmers. After treatment, the effluent is discharged into the Manchester Ship Canal below Barton Locks.

The total volume of sewage delivered at the Works during the year ending March 25, 1908, was 13 360 240 000 gallons, or an average daily flow of 36 704 000 gallons. During the year, the sludge steamer, which carries 1000 tons of sludge, made 177 trips to sea. The total volume of sewage filtered by the various filter beds was 11 583 077 000 gallons, or 86,7 per cent of the total flow, the whole of the unfiltered sewage being treated in the sedimentation tanks. The total area of the works is $434^{1}/_{2}$ acres, of which 279 acres are let to farmers.

The Withington Sewage Works came under the control of the Rivers Committee on the amalgamation of Withington with the City in 1904. They were originally laid out as a sewage farm, but new works for the bacterial treatment of sewage have been in operation for some years. The system of treatment adopted is simple sedimentation followed by the oxidation of the effluent on first and second contact bacteria beds, the resulting effluent being discharged into the Chorlton Brook, a tributary of the River Mersey, and the sludge being trenched into the land.

During the year 1907—1908, the volume of sewage delivered at these works was 1 523 637 477 gallons, which gives an average daily flow of 4 185 817 gallons. The total amount of sludge removed from the tanks was 10 881 tons, equal to 7,1 tons per million gallons.

During the year, 11 848 tons of house refuse were delivered at the Destructor and burnt. The resulting clinker, which is about one third of the refuse, is sold for road making, etc. and during the year 3352 tons were disposed of; glass, iron, tins, etc. picked out of the refuse were also sold. The total area of the land is $81^{1}/_{2}$ acres, 56 of which are under cultivation or let to farmers.

The Moss Side Sewage Works came under the control of the Rivers Committee at the same time as the Withington Works. The method of treatment in operation here is chemical precipitation followed by the filtration of the effluent through land. The system has not proved satisfactory, as it is found impossible to purify large quantities of sewage on the land and it is intended to divert the sewage from the Moss Side Sewage Works to the Davyhulme Sewage Works. The total area of the Moss Side Works is 52 acres.

As the Sewage Works are only trading enterprises to a very slight extent, a few details of a financial character may be given here, so that the matter need not be discussed in any other section. The Davyhulme Works obtained a small revenue in 1907—1908 from the sale of farm produce, grease and scrap metal, from rents of land and sundries, together amounting to £ 1319. — The total cost of the treatment exclusive of interest and repayment of capital, and after deducting the £ 1319 received, amounted to £ 27147 which gives an average cost per million gallons of £ 2. 0. 7 d. The net total cost of the work at Withington Works during the same year 1907—1908, exclusive of interest and the sum devoted to the sinking fund, but after deducting £ 883 received by the sale of produce, of clinkers, etc. and by rents, was £ 4160, or £ 2. 14. 8 d per million gallons treated. The cost of the Moss Side Farm, exclusive of interest and sinking fund charges, was £ 1813 — from which receipts of £ 210 must be deducted giving a net total cost of £ 1603.

The net total cost of conducting the three works, viz: £ 32910, together with interest on all capital borrowed and the sum set aside for sinking fund purposes, had to be met out of the city rates, with the exception of the contributions from Levenshulme, Stretford and Audenshaw Urban District Councils, whose sewage is treated at the Withington and Davyhulme Works by arrangement with the Manchester Corporation. The sum received from these three local authorities in 1907—1908 in respect of the expense of treating their sewage was £ 5131.

Baths and Wash-houses.

The facilites provided by the Baths Committee in twelve buildings situated in different parts of the City, include 25 swimming baths, 512 wash baths, 3 sets of Turkish baths and Russian baths. In addition, there are 10 vapour baths and 2 public wash-houses. In the last named establishments there are 40 washing stalls with the requisite machinery, ironing tables, drying stoves, etc.

At the largest institutions there are three swimming baths,

two for males, first and second class, and one for females. The latter is first class at certain times and second class at others. The ordinary charges for admission to the males' swimming baths are as follows:

1st class — Adults, 4 d; Boys under 14, 2 d
2nd class — Adults, 2 d; Boys under 14, 1 d
2nd class on Wednesdays — 1 d all day.

Scholars over 7 years of age are admitted free into the 2nd class swimming baths, on any day except Saturdays, if in charge of a teacher. Scholars, unaccompanied by a teacher, are admitted to a first class swimming bath for 1 d and to a second-class swimming bath for $1/2$ d. Members of swimming clubs are admitted to a first-class swimming bath for 2 d and to a second class swimming bath for 1 d. Annual, summer-season and winter-season tickets are also issued. In the case of wash baths, the charge is 6 d for a special bath, 4 d for a 1st class, 2 d for a 2nd class and 1 d for a 2nd class on Wednesdays.

The charges for women and girls coincide approximately with those for men and boys.

During the year 1907—1908 the total number of bathers was 1 411 053 made up as follows:

Males' Wash Baths	251 248
Females' Wash Baths	106 018
Males' Swimming Baths	391 547
Females' Swimming Baths	38 181
Turkish	12 447
Scholars paid	194 486
Scholars free	417 126
	1 411 053

The two wash-houses are situated in congested working-class districts, at New Islington and Pryme Street, Ancoats. At Pryme Street, during the year ending March 31, 1908, there were 16 051 washers and the hours worked were 41 776. At New Islington there were 14 622 washers and the hours worked were 48 882. The Baths Committee consider that the wash-houses meet a public need, and are arranging to erect 4 more in different parts of the town.

In what concerns the financial aspect of the baths and wash-houses, no attempt is made to manage them on a remunerative basis.

The Corporation is desirous of encouraging the use of the baths as far as possible, without throwing them entirely free, as a result of which, the better classes would probably be kept away entirely. It is absolutely necessary to differentiate between the lower and the middle classes, if the latter are to use the swimming baths. The tariff is based upon this principle and goes so far as to charge 50 per cent extra for 1st class tickets at the Victoria Baths, which are the most modern and luxuriously fitted. During the year 1907 —1908 the revenue of the Baths Committee from swimming and wash baths was £ 7992, from public wash-houses £ 567 and from other sources £ 780, or a total of £ 9345. The total expenditure of the committee, including interest and sinking fund, was £ 39 008 which comprised £ 28 754 working expenditure and £ 10 254 interest and sinking fund. The deficit, paid from the rates, was £ 29 663, or 76 per cent of the total expenditure.

Cemeteries.

The Manchester Corporation owns four cemeteries with a total area of 230 acres. The oldest is the Philips Park Cemetery acquired in 1864. The Southen Cemetery was purchased in 1872 and the Northern in 1894, whilst the Withington Cemetery was acquired in 1904, at the time when the district of Withington amalgamated with the City. The Cemeteries are managed by a Burial Board, which is subsidized to a small extent out of the City rates. In 1907—1908 the Board had receipts amounting to £ 12 213, whilst its expenditure, including interest and sinking fund charges, amounted to £ 13 680, so that the deficit was approximately £ 1500.

Financial Result of Municipal Trading.

Taking the various trading enterprises, in the widest sense of the expression, in which the Manchester Corporation engages, there are only four which contribute anything directly to the relief of the rates. These departments are the gas, electricity, tramways and markets. The water undertaking just pays its way. The baths and wash-houses, the cleansing department, the housing undertaking and the sewage works are regularly subsidised out of the rates. In the past, the Manchester Ship Canal has proved a very heavy burden, as the Ship Canal Company was unable to pay interest on the Corporation loan of £ 5 000 000, which the City in its turn had borrowed, and on which the annual interest charge was nearly £ 160 000 without taking into account the sum to be set aside for a sinking fund; at one time, consequently, the City rates were increased by 1/— in the £, which is 5 % of the rateable value and under normal conditions $4^1/_6$ % of the actual rent of a house. The Ship Canal rate, as it is called, has gradually been reduced to almost nothing, as the Company is now able to pay most of the annual interest. The accumulated arrears of interest have been converted into $3^1/_2$ % preference shares, on which so far no dividend has been paid. In the future, when the Corporation has paid off a large part, if not all, of the £ 5 000 000 loan, and when it receives interest on the debentures and preference shares which it holds in the Company, a large sum should be available for the relief of the rates, but it will really have been obtained entirely at the expense of a previous generation of ratepayers.

The undertaking managed by the Waterworks Committee has no direct influence upon the municipal finances, as the object of the department at all times is to adjust as far as possible the income to the expenditure. Out of revenue are paid all expenses connected with maintenance and administration, also all repairs and renewals, the balance being employed to meet interest and sinking fund charges. Some years there is a small deficiency, other years there is a small surplus, but whether there be a small loss or a small profit it is carried forward to the next year's accounts and in no way affects the ordinary municipal finances. If the accumulated deficiency, or surplus, becomes considerable, some alteration in the charge for water is made.

On March, 31st, 1906, there was a net deficiency of £ 70 442, but surpluses during the next three years of £ 9947, £ 15 268 and £ 23 983 reduced the net deficiency to £ 21 244 on March 31, 1909. The reduction of the deficiency is partly explained by the increase of the City water rate by 1 d in the £ from April 1, 1908, the domestic water rate being raised from 8 d to 9 d in the pound and the public water rate from 2 d to 3 d in the pound. This was rendered necessary by the increased interest and sinking fund charges, due to capital expenditure in connection with the Thirlmere scheme.

The waterworks may have an indirect influence on the municipal finance, in so far as the Corporation has borrowed on behalf of the department a very large sum of money, for which the Corporation is ultimately responsible and which must tend in any case to raise the rate of interest at which the municipality can borrow in the money market.

The most important trading department of the Corporation, from the point of view of the amount of its appropriation of net profits to be applied in relief of the rates, is undoubtedly the Gas Department. Ever since the Gas Works were taken over by the Corporation from the Commissioners of Police on June 24, 1843, they have been managed on a remunerative basis; there has always been a surplus on the revenue account after paying all operating expenses, interest, sinking fund charges and renewals and repairs. Some of the net profit has been applied in extension of works, some in providing street lighting free of charge to the municipality, but the largest amount has been paid to the Improvement Committee, to the Waterworks Committee, and to the City Fund in relief of rates. During the 65 years that the gas works have been municipalised (from June 24, 1843 till March 31, 1908) the total amount applied in relief of rates was £ 2 858 584, made up as follows:

Paid to Improvement Committee	£ 1 367 641
Paid to Waterworks Committee	166 265
Paid to City Fund	995 476
Street Lighting	329 202
	£ 2 858 584.

Money paid to the Improvement Committee was devoted to town improvements such as public parks, sewers, street paving, buildings etc. The sum paid to the Waterworks Committee was used to reduce water rates. Since 1892, the Corporation pays the Gas Committee for all gas used for street lighting purposes. Since 1888 surplus profits have been paid to the City Fund, thereby reducing taxation. The contributions to the City Fund for the ten years 1899—1908 respectively, were £ 51 200, £ 52 000, £ 51 900, £ 50 000, £ 50 000, £ 70 000, £ 60 000, £ 59 283, £ 60 000, £ 50 000, or a total of £ 553 283 for the ten years which gives an average of £ 55 328 per annum.

After the Gas Department, the department which contributes most largely to the relief of the rates is the Tramways Department. The Corporation operated only part of the system during the years 1901—1902 and 1902—1903 and it is consequently only since then that the full earning capacity has been reached. Each year after meeting all operating expenses, after paying interest on the debt, after devoting the requisite sum to the service of the sinking fund and after setting aside a sum for reserve, renewals and depreciation, there has remained a profit which has been paid into the City Fund in relief of rates. Since the municipalisation of the system, during the seven years 1901—1902 to 1907—1908, the total sum paid by the Tramways Department to the City Fund has been £ 307000, the amounts for the separate years being £ 20000, £ 30000, £ 50000, £ 51000, £ 46000, £ 55000, and £ 55000. On two occasions a sum was transferred from reserve fund, £ 13548 at the end of the first year and £ 5000 at the end of the fourth year, to enable a larger sum to be paid to the City Fund, so as to do away with the necessity of increasing the rates. During the five years that the tramway system has been operated in its entirety by the Corporation, £ 257000 have been contributed to the City Fund, or an average of £ 51400 per annum.

The sums contributed by the Electricity Department in aid of the rates are comparatively small. Although the Department has been operating for 16 years, it has contributed to the City Fund only on eight occasions, a total amount of £ 74964 made up as follows: £ 6964 in 1896; £ 10000 in 1897 and in 1898; £ 12000 in 1899; £ 10000 in 1900; £ 4000 in 1901; £ 10000 in 1908 and £ 12000 in 1909. The average annual contributions to the rates since the Department commenced operations is £ 4685, and since the last ten years £ 3600. The Department has in no occasion been subsidised by the City.

The Market undertakings, considered as a whole, are not merely self-supporting but profitable to a small extent. If the various undertakings are considered separately, it will be found that a good many, including the cold stores and foreign animals wharf, are unremunerative, whilst others, including the abattoirs and markets, are remunerative, the latter much more so than the former. Thus in 1908—1909, after payment of all working expenses, administrative charges, interest on existing loans and sinking fund charges, there was a deficiency of £ 345 on the fish cold stores, of £ 2725 on the meat cold stores and of £ 3215 on the foreign animals wharf, whilst there was a surplus of £ 1319 in connection with the abattoirs and of £ 13417 in connection with the Smithfield and fish markets. The net surplus of the Markets Department was £ 8272.

For twenty years prior to 1906, the Markets Department had yearly contributed a sum of £ 14000 or £ 15000 to the relief of the City rates. Since then, the policy of the Department has undergone an important change. The Committee now realise that part of the money handed over to the City Fund in previous years should have been devoted to the maintenance, repair and renewals of the property of the Department, and during the last four years considerable sums have been spent out of revenue in making the necessary repairs, extensions, etc. Thus the sum paid to the City Fund in aid of rates in 1905—1906 was £ 11000; in 1906—1907 £ 1064; in 1907—1908 £ 2071 and in 1908—1909 £ 7250.

All the Housing schemes within the central parts of the city were designed and carried out for the double purpose of providing houses and of improving the sanitary conditions of the localities by widening and opening out thoroughfares, etc. The actual cost of the several properties purchased by the Corporation is therefore divided between the sanitary improvements account and the housing account [1].

For the purpose of enabling the Committee to judge of the financial results of any particular set of houses, the land actually occupied by the buildings and premises connected therewith is valued at a price fixed by the Council, usually 10/— per sq. yard, the residue of the cost of the land being charged to the sanitary improvement account. This nominal price may be contrasted with the prices actually paid for the land, including unhealthy buildings, which varied from 30/— to £ 5. 6. 9 d per sq. yard.

In the Corporation accounts for each different building scheme

---

[1] This does not apply to the Blackley Estate, which is on the outskirts of the City, nor to the Rochdale Road Dwellings, which were erected on land purchased from the Improvements Committee at a nominal price.

a return is given showing 1. the receipts for rents, 2. the payments for rates, repairs and other outgoings, exclusive of chief rent and debt charges, 3. the net rentals obtained by substracting the expenditure, as indicated, from the receipts. These net rentals are then expressed as a percentage of the total estimated cost, this latter consisting of the price of the buildings plus the nominal value of the land. The percentage is taken as indicating the rate of interest earned by the money invested in the land and buildings. In some years it is very low or even a negative quantity, and in no case can any of the building schemes be described as remunerative, and they are always more or less subsidised out of the rates. It is not the intention of the Corporation that these housing schemes should be self-supporting.

Details of the financial aspects of Municipal Housing are given in the table which follows:

Table showing percentage of net rentals (before payment of chief rents and debt charges) on Total Estimated Cost of various housing schemes.

Building Schemes	Total Estimated Cost (taking land at Committee's valuation)	Percentage of net rental on Total Estimated Cost	Period to which figures relate
	£		Average for:
Oldham Road, No. 2 Block.	66 163	2,42	10 years, 1900—1909
Pollard Street . . .	27 912	0,69	10 years, 1900—1909
Chester Street . . .	16 876	2,89	10 years, 1900—1909
Oldham Road, No. 1 Block.	32 174	3,47	10 years, 1900—1909
Pott Street	19 899	2,08	10 years, 1900—1909
Harrison Street (lodging house)	25 252	0.45	9 years, 1901—1909
Rochdale Road . .	14 574[1]	2,42	3 years, 1907—1909
Blackley Dwellings .	45 315[1]	1,71	4 years, 1906—1909

[1] The land used is valued at the price actually paid in these cases.

The Cleansing Department is essentially one which is subsidised from the city fund, although the total receipts of the department, during the year 1907—1908, amounted to £ 48 850, made up as follows:

Concentrated Manure	£ 11 945
Nightsoil	3 950
Stable manure	1 157
Sweepings	88
Removal of Ashes and Rubbish	334
Mortar	3 141
Old iron	591
Sanitary Soap	56
Horses	472
Disinfecting	5 471
Work done for Sanitary Committee (other than disinfecting)	113
Cleansing markets	4 300
Rents	8 759
Provender supplied to other committees	4 815
Casual	3 647
Bank interest	111
	£ 48 850

Duriug this same year the net cost of the department to the City was £ 143 554, without counting the sum of £ 15 882 devoted to the liquidation of loans.

The Selling Policy of the Municipal Enterprises.

Water. — Although the object of the Water Department is merely to secure sufficient revenue to defray the operating expenses, the cost of maintenance and renewals, the interest on capital borrowed and the sinking fund charges, without any attempt to earn a surplus to be applied to the relief of the rates, the selling policy is somewhat complicated. The Committee have only one commodity to sell, namely water, yet quite a number of different charges are made. In the first place, there is a difference according to whether the water is used within or beyond the limits of the city, the charges being in favor of the Manchester consumers. In the second place, there is a distinction according to whether the water is used for domestic purposes, or for industrial or special purposes. In the former case, the charge is based upon the poor rate assessment, which is five-sixths of the rateable value or real rent of the property; in the latter case, the charge is in proportion to the quantity consumed. Where the water rate is levied, it is so much in the pound, or in other words, a fixed percentage of the poor rate assessment. Where the charge is proportional to the consumption, the price varies according to the quantity consumed; a small amount is paid for at the rate of 2/— per 1000 gallons and the price falls steadily as the quarterly consumption increases, until it reaches 4,85 d per 1000 gallons in the case of a City consumer using more than 3 000 000 gallons in a period of 3 months. In the third place, the domestic water rate on small houses, the rent of which is payable at shorter periods than three months, is 20 per cent lower than the usual water rate[1]. — In these cases, the domestic water rate is charged to the owner, who is allowed a discount of 20 per cent, provided the number of these small houses which he owns is not fewer than three, and provided payment is made on or before October 31st[2], whether the houses be occupied or unoccupied. In the fourth place, there are two different water rates within the city. There is the public water rate, which is at present 3 d in the pound upon the poor rate assessment. It is levied on all property and is payable by the owner. In the second place, there is the domestic water rate, at present 9 d in the pound upon the poor rate assessment. This is levied on dwelling houses only and is payable by the occupier, except where the rent is due at periods of less than three months, when it is payable by the owner, as stated above.

The supply of hydraulic power is paid for according to the quantity of water used, the larger the consumption, the lower the rate.

Gas. The problems associated with the sale of gas are much more complex than those associated with the sale of water. In the first place, it is necessary to take into account the quality of the gas, and, in the second place, to bear in mind that gas is by no means

---

[1] The rents of practically all working-class houses are paid weekly.
[2] That is before six months of the financial year of the Water Department have elapsed.

the only product of a gas works: coke, coal tar and ammoniacal liquor are produced simultaneously with gas, but the ratio between the four products is not fixed but variable. The usual custom is to regard gas as the product of a gas works, and coke, coal tar and ammoniacal liquor as the by-products or residuals. The danger of the conception is, that an outsider is liable to fail to realise the enormous importance of the so called by-products in gas finance. It varies greatly, in some cases the revenue from the sale of by-products is 60 per cent of that derived from the sale of gas; in other cases it is only 20 per cent, or even less.

In Manchester, the revenue derived from the sale of by-products is comparatively small as is shown in the following table, in which the income from the sale of gas, the income from residual products, and the ratio of the latter to the former in terms of percentages, are given for the last five years.

Year ending March 31st	Income from Sale of Gas	Income from Residual Products	Ratio of Column (3.) to col. (2.) in percentages.
1.	2.	3.	4.
	£	£	
1904	613 120	130 843	21,3
1905	573 666	115 288	20,1
1906	582 593	116 973	20,1
1907	601 561	129 341	21,5
1908	621 691	160 999	25,9

In considering the price of the gas sold by the Manchester Corporation, it is necessary to notice in the first place that a difference is made according to whether the gas is supplied within the City or without the City. At one time the difference in favour of Manchester consumers was much more considerable than at present. Prior to 1900, consumers in the near out-townships paid 6 d more per 1000 cubic feet and consumers in the remote out-townships 1 s more than City consumers, but since 1900 all consumers beyond the city boundary pay only 3 d more per 1000 cubic feet than those within it, providing an ordinary meter is employed.

A different and higher scale of charges is in force where the gas is prepaid by means of an automatic meter: 2 s 9 d and 3 s 4 d per 1000 cubic feet within and beyond the City respectively, as compared with 2/3 and 2/6 in the case of ordinary meters. On the other hand, a lower scale of charges is in force where gas is used for power purposes, the price being 1/9 per 1000 cubic feet within the City and 2/— without the City.

The present scale of charges has been in force a few years only, numerous changes having occurred since the inauguration of the works. The price per 1000 cubic feet within the City was 14/— in 1825; it was reduced to 12/— in 1829, to 10/6 in 1831, to 10/— in 1834, to 8/— in 1837, to 7/— in 1840, to 6/— in 1843, to 5/— in 1848, to 4/6 in 1860, to 4/— in 1861, to 3/9 in 1863, to 3/6 in 1864, to 3/2 in 1865, was slightly higher from 1873 to 1877, was reduced to 3/— in 1878, to 2/10 in 1881, to 2/8 in 1882 and to 2/6 in 1890. The movements in the price of gas since that date are indicated in the table given opposite. The large and steady fall in the price of gas from 14/— per 1000 cubic feet in 1825, to 2/6 in 1890 must be ascribed very largely to improvements in the methods of production, and to the economies due to the increase in the scale of production. The most important factor in determining the cost of producing gas, and consequently the selling price, in recent years at least, is the cost of coal. In the table given opposite there is indicated, in addition to the price of gas during the last twenty years, the average cost of coal per ton to the gas department. A casual glance is sufficient to show that the two sets of figures are roughly correlated; in other words, the price of gas tends to move with the price of coal. But there are other influences at work. In the first place, the quantity of gas produced per ton of coal has tended to increase of recent years. In the second place, the illuminating power of the gas has tended to fall. In the last place, the revenue derived from the sale of by-products is tending to rise, not only absolutely, but relatively to the cost of coal and cannel. The result of these three influences should be to lower the price of gas quite apart from movements in the price of coal. Figures illustrating these considerations are also embodied in the table on the opposite page.

As already pointed out, a very important factor which influences the selling price of gas is the revenue obtained from the sale of the by-products. The greater this is, the lower the price of gas. The Manchester Gas Department, like every other gas undertaking,

Table shewing price of gas, coal etc., 1889—1908.

Year ending March 31.	Price of gas per 1000 cu. ft.								Average cost of coal per ton		Gas produced per ton of coal	Illuminating power in candles	Proportion of cost of coal and cannel obtained by sale of residual products
	Within City		Near Out-Townships		Remote Out-Townships		Average of all sold[1]						
	s	d	s	d	s	d	s	d	s	d	cubic ft.		
1889	2	8	3	2	3	8	2	7,50	12	2,05	10 236	20,14	36,72 %
1890	2	6	3	0	3	6	2	5,98	11	11,40	9 826	19,74	39,79 "
1891	2	6	3	0	3	6	2	5,16	12	3,85	9 526	19,26	45,60 "
1892	2	6	3	0	3	6	2	6,76	13	4,10	9 684	19,55	41,23 "
1893	2	6	3	0	3	6	2	6,79	13	7,43	9 957	19,11	32,93 "
1894	2	6	3	0	3	6	2	6,82	16	3,16[2]	9 802	19,04	55,55 "
1895	2	3	3	9	3	6	2	6,81	13	4,49	10 084	19,16	39,62 "
1896	2	3	2	9	3	3	2	3,90	12	3,21	10 025	19,55	37,61 "
1897	2	3	2	9	3	3	2	3,91	11	5,27	10 243	19,16	37,57 "
1898	2	3	2	9	3	3	2	4,23	10	10,38	10 210	19,51	37,57 "
1899	2	3	2	9	3	3	2	3,93	10	9,98	10 445	19,36	41,65 "
1900	2	3	2	6	2	6	2	3,73	11	0,54	10 312	19,40	51,72 "
1901	2	6	2	9	2	9	2	6,05	13	10,28	10 298	18,97	45,00 "
1902	2	9	3	0	3	0	2	9,00	14	6,86	10 663	18,54	34,12 "
1903	2	9	3	9	3	9	2	9,16	12	4,24	10 778	18,25	46,18 "
1904	2	6	2	9	2	7	2	6,78	11	3,65	10 868	17,80	50,09 "
1905	2	4	2	7	2	6	2	4,80	10	8,85	10 967	17,04	46,76 "
1906	2	3	2	6	2	6	2	3,71	10	4,74	10 976	15,30[3]	46,19 "
1907	2	3	2	6	2	6	2	3,36	9	11,81	11 099	17,67	50,99 "
1908	2	3	2	6	2	6	2	3,39	11	4,17	10 948	17,53	53,33 "

[1] By automatic as well as ordinary meters, for power as well as for lighting purposes.
[2] Coal Strike.
[3] By flat flame burner, instead of Metropolitan No. 2 burner.

seeks to obtain the highest possible price for its by-products. The price of coke is determined entirely by the free play of demand and supply, and so far as this by-product is concerned, the Manchester Gas Works are not particularly favorably situated. There is no local industry requiring large supplies, nor is it possible to transport the coke cheaply to places where it is required. The Department fixes prices at each of the gas works and alters them in accordance with movements of the supplies. With an increase in the price of coal, the demand for coke rises and consequently the price of coke is raised.

In 1906—1907 the average cost of coal consumed at the Gas Works was 9 s 11,81 d per ton, whilst the average price obtained for the coke sold was 6 s 8,66 d per ton, or 67 % of the cost of the coal. In 1907—1908 the average cost of coal had risen to 11 s 4,17 d, whilst the average amount realised by coke during the year was 8 s 11,59 d per ton, or 78 % of the cost of the coal.

The tar produced at the different works is sold at prices varying according to a sliding scale which has been in operation for some ten years. It is based upon the selling price, as determined monthly by independent assessors, of the five principle products of tar: naphtha, light oils, creosote, anthracine and pitch. To the value of certain quantities of these products, the quantities varying for each works according to the nature of the tar produced there, is added a sum as remuneration to the purchaser for distilling the tar. As the prices of tar products fluctuate considerably, so consequently does the price of tar. In 1906—1907 the average price realised per ton of coal tar was 20 s 4 d, whilst in 1907—1908 it was only 17 s 11 d.

The third important by-product of the gas works is ammoniacal liquor. Formerly this was sold to distillers, but since 1902 the Gas Committee manufacture sulphate of ammonia on their own account, which has the advantage of securing a considerably wider market. It is sold weekly to the highest bidder, the average price obtained per ton in 1907—1908 being £ 8. 2. 7 d. It is purchased by merchants who ship it abroad for manure.

Electricity Department. From its commencement in 1893, it has had numerous difficulties to contend with. In the first place, there was the competition of the firmly established municipal gas department, the position of which was greatly strengthened by the introduction of the incandescent mantle. In the second place, as electricity was generated only on a very small scale, the cost of production was necessarily high. This alone was sufficient to prevent an extensive use of electricity. Any desire the Department might have had to realise a large profit on a small output was rendered impossible by the terms of the Manchester Electric Lighting Order, which limited the amount of the surplus, or net profits, to five per cent, and the reserve fund to ten per cent on the aggregate capital expenditure.

In the early years of the Department, the limitation with regard to profits was a factor of some importance, but since about 1900 the policy of the Electricity Committee has entirely changed, and their present policy is to sell a very large quantity at a low price yielding only a very small margin of profit. The large use of current for traction purposes has led to a great increase in the scale of production and consequently to an important reduction in the cost of production. At the present time a little under half the current sold by the Electricity Department is purchased by the Tramways Department.

The steady fall in the average price obtained per unit and the decrease in the margin of profit is clearly shown in the table which follows:

Statement showing price of Electricity, percentage of Expenditure to gross revenue, and net profits in different years.

Year ending March 31st	Average price obtained per unit in pence	Percentage of expenditure (including interest and sinking fund charges)	Net profits expressed as percentage of capital expenditure
1895	5,78	80,70	3,78
1896	5,13	70,88	5,22
1897	4,80	67,34	5,99
1898	3,89	76,44	4,05
1899	3,50	76,11	4,04
1900	3,25	88,68	1,72
1901	3,12	96,54	0,47
1902	3,07	94,32	0,75
1903	2,71	95,78	0,58
1904	2,21	97,46	0,36
1905	2,14	98,50	0,21
1906	1,93	95,07	0,73
1907	1,73	92,43	1,13
1908	1,44	94,91	0,80
1909	1,30	96,73	0,47

Rate of charges for electricity since commencement of supply[1].

Date	Lighting	Power
July, 1893	8 d per unit, or 2 d per unit and £ 3 per quarter per unit of demand.	
March, 1895	6 d per unit, or 2 d per unit and £ 3 per quarter per unit of demand.	
September, 1896	6 d per unit, or 1½ d per unit and £ 2. 5. 0 d per quarter per unit of demand.	
September, 1897	5 d per unit, or 1½ d per unit and £ 1. 15. 0 d per quarter per unit of demand.	
September, 1899	5 d per unit, or 1¼ d per unit and £ 1. 15. 0 d per quarter per unit of demand.	As for lighting, or 2½ d per unit, or 1¼ d per unit when maximum demand is used for 48 hours per week.
September, 1901	5½ d per unit, or 1¾ d per unit and £ 1. 15. 0 d per quarter per unit of demand.	As for lighting, or 3 d per unit, or 1¾ d per unit when maximum demand is used for 48 hours per week.
March, 1903		Sliding scale from 1⅞ d per unit down to 1 d per unit according to hours of use.
September, 1905	4½ d per unit, or 1¾ d per unit and £ 1. 15. 0 d per quarter per unit of demand	
March, 1906		1 d per unit when units consumed are 300 or more per E.H.P. per quarter; 1¼ d per unit when less.

[1] Definitions: Unit is short for Board of Trade Unit which is the same as a Kilowatt hour and is equivalent to the consumption of 16 ordinary 16 candle power glow lamps for an hour. One E.H.P. or electric horse power is equal to 746 watts, or for an hour is approximately equal to three quarters of a Board of Trade unit.

Rate of Charges for Electricity — Continued.

Date	Lighting	Power
December, 1907	$3^3/_4$ d per unit, or $1^1/_2$ d per unit and £ 1. 15. 0 d per quarter per unit of demand.	
September, 1908		$1^1/_4$ d per unit when units consumed are below 300 per E.H.P. per quarter; 1 d per unit when units consumed are equal to or above 300 per E.H.P. per quarter; 0,9 d per unit when units consumed are equal to or above 400 per E.H.P. per quarter; 0,8 d per unit when units consumed are equal to or above 500 per E.H.P. per quarter; 0,7 d per unit when units consumed are equal to or above 600 per E.H.P. per quarter. Alternative rate for long hour consumers: 0,33 d per unit and 25 s per quarter per E.H.P. of maximum demand.
March, 1906 . .		Hoists: at a graduating scale of $1^7/_8$ to 1 d per unit.

Since current was first supplied in July, 1893, there have been numerous changes in the scale of charges, all in the direction of a reduction in the prices and of an increased differentiation between current supplied for lighting purposes, and current supplied for power purposes. In the early years no difference was made between light and power consumers, but it was soon realised that the latter could be supplied at a much lower price owing to the steady nature of their demand, and the tariff was altered accordingly. Above is given a table indicating in detail the changes in the charges since the inauguration of the Department.

Tramways. The two principal considerations which have influenced the Corporation in fixing tram fares are 1. that passengers should pay roughly in proportion to the distance travelled and 2. that the penny passenger is the mainstay of the system. At no time does there appear to have been a movement in favour of a universal fare which is practically unknown in the United Kingdom. On the other hand, the Tramways Committee have quite realised that cheap fares are one of the best means of combating overcrowding of the population in the central portions of the City by making it possible for working people to live farther away from the centre. At the same time, working-class people cannot afford to pay large fares. This has been taken into account in drawing up the scale of charges which is so arranged that, roughly, the lower the fare, the greater the distance proportionately which can be travelled for the fare; in other words, the small consumers are favoured as against the big consumers, apart from the halfpenny stage which is considered separately below. As a general rule, the stages commencing from the centre of the town are longer than the stages at the same price along the route. For purposes of comparison as between the different fares, the average length of each stage on the Corporation Tramway System is indicated below:

Fare	Average length of stage		Pence per mile
d	miles	yards	d
$1/2$	0	1431	0,614
1	2	372	0,452
$1^{1}/_{2}$	2	1403	0,536
2	3	1329	0,532
$2^{1}/_{2}$	4	850	0,557
3	5	243	0,583
$3^{1}/_{2}$	5	1360	0,606
4	6	984	0,609
$4^{1}/_{2}$	7	1251	0,583
5	8	935	0,586
$5^{1}/_{2}$	9	765	0,582

At the present time there is a proposal before the Corporation, somewhat to reduce the long-distance fares, as an experiment on one route has shown, that this can be done without adversely affecting the revenue. If the proposals are put into force, the halfpenny and penny stages will remain as before and the remaining stages will be as follows[1]:

[1] These changes were introduced on Oct. 31. 1909.

Fare	Average length of proposed stage		Pence per mile
d	miles	yards	
1½	3	193	0,482
2	4	57	0,495
2½	4	1561	0,511
3	5	1203	0,527
3½	6	1024	0,531
4	7	1251	0,518
4½	8	935	0,527
5	9	765	0,529

The question of halfpenny fares is one of great interest in Manchester. At present they exist only on circular and cross routes, the average length of the stage being 1431 yards, or at the rate of 0,614 pence per mile. There has been quite recently an agitation in favour of adopting halfpenny stages on the main routes radiating from the centre of the town. In considering the proposal, it is necessary to bear in mind that the penny passenger is the mainstay of the tramway system, somewhat more than two thirds of all the passengers carried paying a penny fare. Those unacquainted with tramway finance are inclined to argue, that if a passenger can be carried two miles for one penny, it ought to be possible to carry him half that distance for a halfpenny. This leaves out of consideration the fact that there are a large number of short distance penny riders. Statistical inquiries show that 35 per cent of the penny passengers travel only a mile or less, and it is estimated that the adoption of one mile halfpenny stages would have the effect of transferring 50 per cent of the penny passengers to the halfpenny class and would result in a reduction in revenue of £ 107 020 per annum. To make up for this loss of revenue, 51 millions of additional halfpenny passengers would have to be carried per annum, which alone would necessitate a large increase in the number of cars, and consequently increased working expenses and fixed charges, for the same revenue. There appears to be little doubt, that the whole profit of the undertaking would be wiped out, and a substantial subsidy required from the rates were one mile halfpenny stages adopted. Whilst three-quarters of a mile halfpenny stages would occasion less loss of revenue, it is estimated that they could not be a financial success. This contention is supported by a concrete example of the financial effect of the adoption of three-quarter mile halfpenny stages on the circular route, which forms important cross country connections between all the main routes radiating from the centre of the City. There are carried on the circular route cars 33 per cent more passengers per mile than are carried on the average on the other routes, yet the income does not cover the expenditure.

The Tramways Committee have considered the matter very carefully and are opposed even to half-mile halfpenny stages on the main routes, as certain to cause loss of revenue, and as likely to increase the inconvenience of the public paying a penny and higher fares, during the rush hours in the morning and evening when the cars are already crowded.

Municipal and Private Trading.

In Manchester the opportunities of contrasting the working of municipal and private trading are very limited. There is no undertaking of any particular kind which is partly in municipal and partly in private hands; nor is it possible, with a single exception, to compare conditions before and after municipalisation. As far as gas and electricity are concerned, there were no supplies prior to the inauguration of undertakings by the local authority. The water supply and the management of the markets were municipalised over fifty years ago, and the complete change of conditions would make any comparisons futile, even were it possible to obtain information about these undertakings when they were still in private hands. Any contrast between municipal and private trading appears to be limited to the tramways, in the case of which municipal operation was substituted for private operation during the years 1901 to 1903.

Horse trams first began to run in Manchester in 1877. The tracks were laid by the Corporation and leased to a Private Company for 21 years. In the "nineties" there were $56^1/_2$ miles of track (route mileage $32^1/_2$) for which the Company paid a rent of £ 22 500 per annum. Out of this, the Corporation had to pay interest and sinking fund charges on the capital borrowed, some £ 171 000, which allowed on an average £ 4500 per annum to be paid in relief of the rates. When the Corporation took over the working of the tramway system they adopted a well defined policy, which may be summarised under three heads.

1. To benefit the travelling public by providing more rapid and cheaper transit facilities.

Electric traction was substituted throughout the system for horse traction and the fares were greatly reduced. The fares charged by the Corporation in 1909, as compared with those charged by the old Tramways Company show an average reduction of 40 per cent; if the passengers now using the cars were charged fares at the same rates as obtained in the Company days, they would have to pay £ 500000 per annum more than they do at present.

2. To benefit the rate payers by making contributions in aid of the rates out of the profits of the undertaking.

The total amount paid over to the City Fund in relief of the rates out of the profits of the undertaking during the past eight years (1901—1909) has been £ 377000 or an average of £ 47125 per year, which is ten times as much as the annual average sum paid in relief of the rates by the Company. In addition to this, the Department pays to the City, by way of rates on the tramway track and depots, the sum of £ 27000 per annum, as compared with £ 8000 per annum paid by the old Company. The Department also maintains out of its revenue the whole of the paving between the tramway lines and for 18 inches on the outer sides thereof — in other words, roughly half the cost of maintaining the carriage-ways of the principal streets of the City and suburbs falls upon the tramways department.

3. To benefit the employees by granting better conditions of service.

The hours of labour have been reduced from 70 to 54 per week, whilst the wages per hour have been increased 63 per cent in the case of guards and 43 per cent in the case of drivers.

The total cost to the Department of these concessions amounts to about £ 50000 per annum.

These various concessions distributed between the ratepayers, the travelling public and the employees have been conferred without in any way undermining the financial stability of the undertaking, as a substantial depreciation and renewals fund has been accumulated (amounting to £ 400000 on March 31st, 1909), in addition to the gradual liquidation of the debt by means of the sinking fund (on March 31st, 1909, £ 232 000 had been set aside for this purpose, the total amount of capital borrowed in connection with the undertaking being £ 1 701 000).

General relation of Town Authorities to Municipal Trading.

As several of the most important trading enterprises, such as the supplies of gas and water and the ownership and management of the markets, have been in municipal hands since the formation of the City Council, or since somewhere about that time, it is necessary, in order to ascertain the attitude of the local authority towards municipal trading, to study the actions of the Council in connection with the municipalisation of the electricity supply and of the tramway service which have occurred within comparatively recent years.

In 1881 the Manchester Corporation Gas Committee applied to Parliament for authority to erect a generating station and to lay mains in certain streets. Their application was refused on the ground that no authority should be granted by special act prior to the passage of a general law which was shortly to be introduced into Parliament. Almost immediately after the enactment of the Electric Lighting Act in 1882, the City Council unanimously resolved to apply to the Board of Trade for a provisional order authorizing the establishment of a municipal plant. The Board of Trade insisted upon conditions which were not acceptable to the City and nothing came of the proposal. Until 1889 no further attempt was made to supply the City with electricity. In that year six companies gave notice to the Council, as required by the statute, of their intention to apply to the Board of Trade for the necessary authority to supply current. At this juncture the Gas Committee recommended that another attempt should be made to secure powers, and a special meeting of the Council unanimously decided to promote a provisional order, which was issued by the Board of Trade and approved by Parliament in 1890. The undertaking, which first supplied current in 1893, was originally managed by the Gas Committee, but in 1897 a separate Electricity Committee was appointed.

The municipalisation of the electricity supply may be ascribed to two causes: on the one hand, to a desire to supply electric current in the town at a time when there appeared to be no prospect of private enterprise undertaking the supply, and on the other hand, to a wish to prevent a private company from encroaching upon a field of enterprise which Parliament had decided was suitable, under proper conditions, for municipal management.

The first Manchester Tramways were opened in 1877. The Tramways Act, 1870, permitted municipal construction of the track, but not municipal management. Consequently the Corporation built the tramway and leased it for 21 years to a Company. In February, 1895, a special Committee of the Council was appointed, by a vote of 35 to 10, to consider and report upon the desirability of municipal operation. Eight months later a report was made, recommending that powers to operate be secured from Parliament, not so much with the idea that they would actually be exercised, but to place the City in a position where it could secure good terms from the Company. At a meeting of the owners and ratepayers held to secure permission to promote a bill, the recommendation was rejected. The Special Committee reconsidered the matter, and for the following reasons among others repeated its recommendation that power to operate be obtained from Parliament: a) to secure a better service, especially the introduction of mechanical traction; b) to obtain lower fares; c) to secure for the City more complete control of its streets and their monopoly uses; d) to improve the conditions of labour; e) to extend the lines with a view to making the suburban areas easily accessible; f) to transfer from the Company's shareholders to the public the profits of the public patronage of the tramway service.

In November, 1896, the Council voted to promote a bill to obtain power to operate and to use mechanical traction. This was approved by the owners and ratepayers, and parliamentary sanction was obtained. In 1898, by a vote of 68 to 0, the Council decided definitely to adopt electricity, to operate the lines itself and to make agreements with certain outside local authorities for the operation of their lines in connection with the Manchester system. An Act was passed in 1899 conferring the necessary authority. After much negociation, an agreement was made with the Company providing that all leases in Manchester should terminate on May 31, 1902, and that the City should have the right to reconstruct and operate any line before that date, the payment for this privilege being the average net profit of the Company per mile of track. The City began to operate the first lines in 1901, but did not get full possession of the system until March 31st, 1903.

In view of the numerous trading enterprises engaged in by the City and the way in which their scope has been extended from time to time, there can be no doubt that the Town Council, as a whole, is in favour of a large measure of Municipal Trading; on the other hand, there are doubtless individual members, generally connected more or less closely with industries affected by municipal competition, who are opposed to it, although very possibly they refrain from openly stating their views, as tending to make them unpopular with a majority of the electors, who are proud of the numerous undertakings managed by the Local Authority.

Printed by Libri Plureos GmbH
in Hamburg, Germany